If you wish to experience  the kind Jesus Christ intended for His followers, then prayerfully read this book. Keep your heart and mind open to what God's Spirit is saying. The following transformation will produce the kind of compelling model others will emulate, and our world will see the real Christ.

    John Tolle, Pastor, Crosstown Church, Thousand Oaks, CA

The Incarnational Church is a must read for anyone wanting to mobilize their church and take seriously Jesus' command to love our neighbors. This book will wake you up from complacency and ignite your passion to see your neighbors and neighborhood transformed by Jesus. I highly recommend it and will use it as a resource in our church.

    Joe White, Pastor, Neighborhood Church, Fresno, CA

Lynn Cory is not just one of the contributors to the neighborhood movement. He's one of the catalysts. His latest book, *The Incarnational Church*, will challenge you, inspire you, and give you practical tools to begin neighboring right where you live. While many books point to reasons we *should* neighbor, Lynn goes beyond the *should* to give real-life examples plus practical steps to get you started. You will begin a journey with your neighbors not driven by guilt or strategy, but rather led by the Spirit's incredible desire to see people come to the Father through the Son.

    Tom Anthony, Co-founder of The Neighborhood Collective, Minister of Community Life at Oak Hills Church, San Antonio, TX

Lynn Cory's book, *The Incarnational Church*, is akin to the "shot across the bow" or the proverbial "wake-up call" for church leaders across this great country. The neighboring movement is here, blessed by God and positively impacting neighborhoods and communities in both urban and rural settings. Lynn's admonition to embrace the Whole Church . . . the Incarnational Church . . . to release the people of God into their neighborhoods . . . to be like Jesus in both word and deed . . . is compelling. This book is nothing short of a call for all godly leaders in both large and small congregations to realize that relationships built through neighboring are at the core of what God is doing in this present season.

Jim Lloyd, The Bridge, Fresno, CA

If you're looking for ways to increase your church membership . . . if you're looking for new programs to attract more Christians to your church . . . this book is *not* for you. However, if you're looking for ways to get your church involved with Christ's greatest mandate to his people . . . if you're seeking means by which everyone at your church can naturally share the Good News with their next-door neighbor . . . then this book is a must. With his simple, yet practical approach, my dear friend, Lynn Cory, shows us all the importance of completing the task of the Great Commission through loving one neighbor at a time.

Shah Afshar, Founder, Shazam Factor

It is vital for congregations small and large, old and new, to recover the intended purpose of Church by becoming "fully obedient to that ancient mandate, no matter the cost." And what is that ancient mandate? To love our neighbors. As soon as I scanned the table of contents, I knew this was an important text for the learning communities of the John 17, city-focused, movements taking root across our nation and globally. In an era when leaders of the Church are talking, rightly so, of community transformation, Lynn's message of incarnation is critical. He presents a simple and strategic rethinking that is both biblical and practical. And his insights are the result of love. His love for the Lord and His Word. His love for the Church and her mission. His love for the community and our neighbors.

Phil Miglioratti, National Facilitator of Cities/Communities Ministries, Mission America Coalition

Lynn Cory has once again served as Christ's messenger. In *The Incarnational Church* Lynn effectively reminds us of the primacy of the scriptural mandates to love God and our neighbors. He shares a biblical perspective gained after years of pastoral service, along with the wisdom of a pioneering practitioner in an effort to help us better grasp a vision for reaching our communities one neighbor at a time. The case studies help us to discover practical insights to live the essential Christian life of radical love for both God and neighbors.

Bruce Zachary, Pastor, Calvary Nexus, Camarillo, CA

Lynn Cory captures the stories of those already on the journey toward becoming *The Incarnational Church*. This book will inspire you, challenge you, and frustrate you as it casts vision for the future of Our Lord's Church in your city. As a leader, I believe it is time to move away from the attractional model of church growth toward that which Jesus always intended—a relational, unified, loving picture of Jesus to those in our neighborhoods.

Andrew Burchett, Pastor, Neighborhood Community Church, Chico, CA

A couple of years ago, I had the privilege of sitting at a table with Reggie McNeal, author and missional leadership specialist for the Leadership Network. We talked about how the missional-Church conversation produced an abundance of academic resources, but lacked the "nuts and bolts" necessary to advance the Christian movement in the Western hemisphere. Well . . . the book you now hold in your hand represents those nuts and bolts! Lynn is a practitioner. Each page contains real-life-and-church stories to inspire and equip pastors with practical, incarnational insights and ministry approaches that will enable and unleash churches to work together and reach their cities with the transforming love and power of God one neighborhood at a time.

Jeff Fischer, Pastor, Hope Chapel of the Valley, Canoga Park, CA

The Incarnational Church is an excellent book for capturing the vision of the body of Christ uniting with God to accomplish His redemptive plan in the earth. This book is a must read for every Christian leader! Pastor Lynn Cory paints an excellent picture in each chapter, testimony, and story to illustrate what it will be like when pastors and local churches unite their efforts to reclaim our neighborhoods and cities for Christ. This book offers a brilliant snapshot of "The Power of Presence," that makes the greatest impact in missional ministry as the Whole Church demonstrates the love of Christ and the power of the Gospel message as we dwell among those who do not know Him!

Dr. Linda Marcell, Founder, Agape Global Missions
Professor at The King's University, Inglewood, CA

When I finished reading this excellent book, I thought about how much Lynn Cory has influenced my life. From the first time we met, he taught me the importance of pastors reaching out to other pastors by living this out himself. I imitated him. When Lynn introduced me to the work and friendship of Dallas Willard, I imitated him. When Lynn started hearing from the Lord about neighboring and living this out in his own life, I imitated him. I can't give a higher endorsement than to encourage you to imitate him, too.

>**Dana Hanson**, Pastor, LifeHouse Church, Northridge, CA
>Author, *Reboot: 70 Life Lessons of Dallas Willard*

The Incarnational Church is about getting back to the most foundational and organic way God has designed for His church communities to live. This book is about adventuresome relationship, missional lifestyle, unity among churches in our neighborhoods, and community transformation. Its focus is on living out the second half of what our Lord told us is the supreme commandment: loving our neighbors . . . our literal neighbors. Unfortunately, rare is the pastor or church leader who demonstrates for us how this is done. For many years Lynn Cory has been loving his neighbors and showing others how to do it. The results have been revolutionary.

>**Dr. Glen A. Taylor**, Lead Pastor, Vineyard Pasadena Community Church, Pasadena, CA, Adjunct professor of Hebrew and Old Testament, Talbot School of Theology

Lynn is a pioneer in neighborhood ministry, which he does under the guidance of the Lord. This is not theory. He lives it. Lynn is on the crest of a wave that seems to be coming to the Church in the United States. *The Incarnational Church* is both biblical and practical. It presents what churches and cities are doing to help Christians love others. I have learned much from this book and so will you.

>**Alan Doswald**, Executive Director, Evangelicals for Social Action, Fresno, CA

Neighboring seems to be "trending" in churches across America. Lynn, however, shares from a deep conviction of prayer and an attempt to follow what the Father is doing. He adds a spiritual dimension, which is often lacking in our attempt to love those near us. Lynn has mentored our Loving our Neighbors movement in Fresno, both in person and with his first book. This second book continues with practical stories of how this is actually happening in various cities.

> **Paul Haroutunian**, Project Director, Loving Our Neighbors, ESA Love INC, Fresno, CA

The Incarnational Church is a must read for anyone who has a desire to make a difference in their community. Lynn Cory is one of the founders of the neighboring movement, and his work over the years has laid the foundation for much of what I am doing today. This book is chock-full of practical tools and ideas that will help you engage the people who God has placed around you. I can't recommend it enough!

> **Dave Runyon**, Co-author of *The Art of Neighboring*

Don't miss out! The Greatest Commandment offers the most joy: Love God *wholeheartedly*, and love your neighbors *well*. How? Buy this compelling sequel to Lynn Cory's first book. Read what he says. Underline the most meaningful statements. Begin praying through them. And start living the life God offers you!

> **David Sanford**, Executive Editor, *Holy Bible: Mosaic* (Tyndale House Publishers)

THE INCARNATIONAL CHURCH

Catching Jesus' Radical Approach
for Advancing His Kingdom

LYNN CORY
WITH LYLE RANDLES

© 2017 by Lynn Cory

All rights reserved. No part of this publication may be reproduced in any form without written permission from Lynn Cory. lynncory@neighborhoodinitiative.org

ISBN 13: 978-1979743655

Cover design by Nadine Erickson

Unless otherwise identified, all Scripture quotations in this publication are taken from the *Holy Bible, New International Version*® (NIV®). Copyright © 1973, 1978, 1984, 2011 by Biblica, Inc. ® Used by permission of Zondervan. All rights reserved worldwide. www.zondervan.com. The "NIV" and "New International Version" are trademarks registered in the United States Patent and Trademark Office by Biblica, Inc.® Other versions used include: *THE MESSAGE* (MSG), copyright © 1993, 1994, 1995, 1996, 2000, 2001, 2002, used by permission of NavPress Publishing Group; the New American Standard Bible® (NASB), copyright © 1960, 1962, 1963, 1968, 1971, 1972, 1973, 1975, 1977, 1995 by The Lockman Foundation, used by permission.

Printed in the United States of America

Dedicated to you, dear jo Cory. You are my precious gift from God, and I deeply love you. You have shown me what it is to love your neighbor as yourself in every setting of our life together. What a blessing you are to me and to everyone you touch.

Contents

	Acknowledgments	1
	A Tribute to Dallas Willard	2
	Foreword by Lyle Randles	4
	Introduction	7
	Collectively Living as Jesus Did	
	Reformation	

SECTION 1 Moving Away from the Attractional Model 15

CHAPTER 1	Restoring Jesus' Intention for His Church	17
CHAPTER 2	Seeing the Church with New Eyes	23
CHAPTER 3	Take Off that Old Garment	27
CHAPTER 4	Establishing Authentic Relationships	33
CHAPTER 5	Let's Stop Being "Churchy"	37
CHAPTER 6	Let's Move Toward Being "Home-Centered"	41
CHAPTER 7	Dones and Nones	45
CHAPTER 8	Let's Take Off the Business Suit	53
CHAPTER 9	Captivated with the Unity	59
CHAPTER 10	Let's Play as a Team	63

SECTION 2 Becoming the Incarnational Church 71

CHAPTER 11	Neighboring Is a Move of God	73
CHAPTER 12	God Initiates a City Movement	77
CHAPTER 13	Do What the Father's Doing	85
CHAPTER 14	War Room	93
CHAPTER 15	Sustained Season of Prayer	97
CHAPTER 16	God Moves at the Speed of Relationship	103
CHAPTER 17	There Is No One Way To Do This	107

SECTION 3	**Stories of the Lord's Incarnational Work in Cities**	**117**
CHAPTER 18	The Lord's Work in the Lord's Way	119
CHAPTER 19	Pioneering a Citywide Neighboring Movement and Beyond	121
CHAPTER 20	Starting a Neighboring Movement in a Neighborhood	127
CHAPTER 21	Turning a Church Small Group Loose in Their Own Neighborhood	131
CHAPTER 22	Starting a Neighboring Movement in a House Church Network	135
CHAPTER 23	Planting a Church with a Neighboring Approach	139
CHAPTER 24	Starting a Citywide Neighborhood Movement	145
CHAPTER 25	The Fresno Story… "Loving Our Neighbors"	149
CHAPTER 26	Seeding Neighborhood Ministry into the San Fernando Valley	153
CHAPTER 27	One Pastor's Journey into Neighborhood Ministry	159
SECTION 4	**Join the Journey**	**165**
CHAPTER 28	On the Journey	167
CHAPTER 29	Starting the Journey	175
CHAPTER 30	Joining the Father in the Neighboring Movement	189
	Notes	193

Acknowledgments

I am deeply indebted to the Lord for His faithfulness in putting into words what I could have never expressed without Him. Thank you, Lord, for Your abundant grace in sharing Your heart with Your people.

I am grateful to the Lord for encouraging me to invite Lyle Randles into the process of editing The Incarnational Church… his prowess in writing, his heart for the subject matter, and his friendship have been invaluable.

I thank God for those friends who have caught and whole heartedly devoted themselves to our Lord's Greatest Commandment…their stories and contributions to The Incarnational Church and neighboring have enriched the book immensely. Thank you for your investment in neighboring and your contributions: Dave Runyon, Shawn and Carla Caldwell, Jim Lloyd, Glen Taylor, Joe White, Andrew Burchett, Paul Haroutunian, Alan Doswald, Jeff Fischer, Tom Anthony, John Tolle, Shah Bruce Zachary, Linda Marcell, Tyler Lennon, Phil Miglioratti, David Sanford, Fred West, Rick McMichael, Bill Dwyer, and Bob and Kathy Leduc.

I am indeed grateful for those who faithfully prayed for me and the writing of The Incarnational Church…Anthony Rodriguez, Jan Enright, Martha Bellamy, Domingo Cabral, Roberto and Sharon Munoz~Flores, Eva Case, Greg Stanley, Rita Humm, Julie Herzog, and many others.

I am thankful to Nadine Erickson for her labor of love on the cover design…what a blessing you have been through the years with Neighborhood Initiative.

Thank you, Kris Wallen, for once again taking the ball to the finish line…I am so grateful that I could pass this new book off to your capable hands for publication.

A Tribute to Dallas Willard

I am deeply grateful to my dear friend Dr. Dallas Willard, whose life and teachings led me into experiencing the best life, life in the easy yoke with Jesus, and a conviction that Jesus' Great Commission is central for His Church today.

Dallas Willard was always an incredible support to me throughout the initial development of Neighborhood Initiative. On one occasion he said to me, "If you keep moving forward with what you are doing, then we will see revival and awakening." He said to me on two occasions, "Don't stop what you are doing!" In the early days I would often think of these words, not so much as from Dallas, but as words of encouragement from the Lord. At one of our breakfasts together, I told him that I was writing a book on Neighborhood Initiative. I told him that I was going to give it the title Neighborhood Initiative. He said, "No, give it the title *Neighborhood Initiative and the Love of God*." His title change served to open my eyes to a deeper realization that Neighborhood Initiative is God's profound work, and I seeded this understanding throughout the book. Writing the book flowed after his important suggestion.

In September 2012, Dallas was scheduled to speak at one of our Neighborhood Initiative conferences for pastors and leaders, but because he was recovering from surgery he was unable to join us. From his hospital bed, he said, "I want to speak to the pastors!" When he was home recovering, a pastor friend, Leroy Chavez, and I videoed what we called "A Heart-Felt Word to Pastors and Leaders." When Dallas finished speaking I said, "Dallas, that was only fifteen minutes!" He responded, "I have said everything I need to say; it's from my heart." I encourage you to read or listen to all that Dallas had to say that day on the subject of loving our neighbors. The transcription of his 15-minute message is in the front of the book *Neighborhood Initiative and the Love of God*, entitled, "A Challenge from Dallas Willard"[1], and the video can be found on the Neighborhood Initiative website (neighborhoodinitiative.org). As you will learn, he gave high praise to the "Neighborhood Initiative Under Christ" and encouraged pastors and leaders to take the lead through their teaching.

Dallas Willard certainly influenced my thinking about what is needed in the church today. He longed for the church to become more incarnational, and it was this longing of his that served to help inspire both the ministry of Neighborhood Initiative as well as the book you now hold in your hands. Like so many others, Dallas was looking for a church that was intentional about actively loving its neighbors, one that was committed to living out Jesus' command: "Love one another. As I have loved you, so you must love one another. By this everyone will know that you are my disciples, if you love one another" (John 13:34–35 NIV).

Foreword

> For the whole Law is fulfilled in one word, in the statement,
> "You shall love your neighbor as yourself."
> —Galatians 5:14 NASB

The biblical mandate to love our neighbors has always raised some interesting questions in my mind: What would happen if followers of Jesus actually began living in such a manner as to demonstrate the love of God toward their neighbors? What would that look like, and what would be the impact upon those living in our communities?

Surely, there is nothing new about loving one's neighbor. The concept is older than Christianity itself. We find it firmly rooted amongst God's commands to Moses (Leviticus 19:18), and it is clear from both the biblical record as well as Church history that Jesus and His disciples took this command quite seriously. But do we, His Church, take this command as seriously today as our brothers and sisters did in the past?

In his first book, *Neighborhood Initiative and the Love of God*, Lynn Cory lovingly and humbly addressed both the significance and the impact of living our lives in accordance with God's command. The world around us is in desperate need, longing to understand if life offers any meaning in the midst of so much pain and suffering. When we, Jesus' followers, openly demonstrate the same love to others that we received from Christ, hope is restored. Light begins to shine in the darkness. Life can indeed take on meaning and significance.

Thus Lynn points toward the importance of all disciples living in such a manner as to fulfill the great commandment to love our neighbors. But in doing so, might this not result in some changes? If we begin to focus attention on those *outside* the walls of our churches, might not the way we conduct ourselves *inside* the church change as well?

There is a movement spreading across this country of ours . . . a movement that emphasizes the importance of re-igniting that passion to love our neighbors. It's sprouting up in many different forms, adapting to local environments and culture. In some neighborhoods, it is represented by people from the same church reaching out to those in need. In other communities we find several churches coming together in unity in an effort to reach the unreached with the love of God. But wherever it blossoms, the DNA is always the same—people loving their neighbors as Christ has loved them.

Yet the question remains: Will this movement lead to change in the way that we do church? Is it possible that some sort of reformation might be in the works?

The Incarnational Church has been written from the premise that God is effecting a great change within the Body of Christ. Lynn and many others sense a change in seasons. The drumbeat that accompanies the spiritual battles of this age appears to have increased. The cost of discipleship seems to be on the rise. The clouds of war are certainly darkening.

How then is the church to respond to the changes around us? Are we to retreat into our bunkers and hunker down, or are we to lovingly advance in the attempt to proclaim the kingdom of God to as many as possible?

From Lynn's perspective, there is only one response to the world's current condition: We must become fully obedient to that ancient mandate, no matter the cost. And if change within the Church becomes necessary, then let us choose obedience over tradition and personal comfort. Let us take up the Royal Law to which our brother James referred (James 2:8), and for the sake of those who do not know the love of God, throw ourselves into the breach with a willingness to make whatever changes might be necessary in order that our neighbors would not only come to know the love of Christ, but would themselves become disciple makers in His name.

Lyle Randles
Chairman, Life Connections International

Introduction

Collectively Living as Jesus Did
"It's Not My Church!"

I received a call from Andrew Burchett, a pastor friend of mine from Chico, California. Andrew is the pastor of a large congregation with many vibrant young people and young families. Ironically, the church is called Neighborhood Church. He had called to ask if I would meet with a group of pastors from his city in order to introduce them to Neighborhood Initiative.

A year earlier, I had met with Andrew to talk with him about Neighborhood Initiative. It was a Sunday afternoon after a busy day for him. We both sat down in his office to talk about the possibilities of NI for his congregation. At the time, Andrew was already very involved with people in his own neighborhood, and what I shared about moving his church toward actively loving their neighbors was just what he was looking for. He embraced it immediately. As we finished our conversation, I told him that it would be important to pull back on the number of programs in his church, so those in his congregation would have time to spend with their neighbors. I was quite surprised at his quick response. He said, "No problem there; *this* is what we will be doing from now on."

This kind of movement—a return to our neighborhoods, so to speak—is not only happening in Chico, but in cities across our country. There is a move of God afoot. It is not breaking out in just one location or even a few. God is launching something that is sweeping through His people, bringing new life to His Church, and touching lives all across the country.

Originally, I had planned to include this book with *Neighborhood Initiative and the Love of God*, but after some consideration I realized it needed to be a separate book. The first book primarily focused on the individual believer and how one can become incarnational in one's own neighborhood. My conviction is that if believers do not start by loving their actual neighbors (of course, it starts first by loving those in their own household) then there will always be a certain disconnect. How can we love people over there if we don't love those just outside our doors? If we love our actual neighbors then we will begin to show the love of Jesus in the natural flow of our lives. Our neighborhoods become the training ground, if you will, for loving people wherever we go. Of course, this starts with a divine work of God as one experiences His presence, observes what He is doing, and then joins Him in His work.

In this book, the focus is on the *Whole Church* in every city becoming collectively incarnational. That is, the corporate body of Christ working together as one to replicate the life and ministry of Jesus in the cities and neighborhoods where He has placed us.

Often church-goers are viewed by those outside as people who are out of touch and judgmental. Because we have chosen to distance ourselves both physically and relationally, they perceive us as having a "holier than thou" attitude. Maybe they are right! However, Jesus immersed Himself with those from every walk of life, and He was loved by the non-religious (sinners and tax gathers) people of His day. This gives some insight as to why Mahatma Gandhi asserted, "I like your Christ. I do not like your Christians. Your Christians are so unlike your Christ." We need to embrace the One we are following and live together as He did.

The Incarnational Church speaks primarily to pastors and

leaders in the church about what the Lord is doing in His Church today. It is moving away from the "my church" perception and heartily acknowledging that it is His Church. It is comprehending that He evaluates His Church geographically, city by city (Revelation 2 and 3). It is about pastors, leaders, and congregations working together as "one" in a city with a single purpose, to show the love of God and reveal the Gospel of the Kingdom to those in our communities.

Reformation
"Churches without Borders"

In my last conversation with Dallas Willard he said to me in reference to Neighborhood Initiative, "This is our only answer." I responded, "It's a real faith walk."

Why, you might ask, do I view Neighborhood Initiative as a walk of faith? Because I view ministering in the neighborhood as countercultural to the American method of doing church. For years, the mantra of the American church has been "y'all come." In contrast to this, Neighborhood Initiative is "y'all go." Pastors and leaders of American churches operate, for the most part, independently of one another. Neighborhood Initiative sees the need for them to work together for the common cause of advancing God's kingdom, one neighborhood at a time. Having done church differently for so many decades, accepting this new paradigm for the church may not be an easy thing for pastors to embrace. Having been in the pastorate myself for so many years, I am not unsympathetic. After all, it is the mode of operation that we all inherited. However, I firmly believe the Lord is bringing about a reformation to His Church. He wants to restructure things by knitting us together as a single Body. The apostle Paul touches on this when he writes: "From Him the whole body, joined and held together by every supporting ligament, grows and builds itself up in love, as each part does its work." (Ephesians 4:16 NIV) The Lord is joining His body together in love for the great work He wants to do through us in our communities. The supporting ligaments are at work in His Church today, through those who are called by God to be connectors in the body of Christ, so that together we will carry out the work of Jesus in our cities.

When I first moved into Neighborhood Initiative I didn't realize that "reformation" was what the Lord had in mind. Think about it. If we begin to love our actual neighbors then we will probably encounter people from other congregations who just happen to live in our neighborhoods. Are we going to avoid them, or are we going to invite them to join us in loving our neighbors as ourselves? If we are obedient, we will submit to His commandment: "A new command I give you: Love one another. As I have loved you, so you must love one another. By this everyone will know that you are my disciples, if you love one another" (John 13:34–35). Philip Yancey points out in *Vanishing Grace*, "When I ask, 'Tell me the first word that comes to your mind when I say *Christian*,' not one time has someone suggested the word *love*. Yet without question that is the proper biblical answer. 'As I have loved you, so you must love one another,' Jesus commanded His disciples at the Last Supper. He said the world will know we are Christians—and, moreover, will know who He is—when His followers are united in love."[2]

I believe the Lord has us in a corner with this neighboring thing. He is calling us to love those from other churches in our own neighborhoods as He has loved us. This is reformation. He is calling His Church to become "churches without borders." This may be threatening to some, but this is where the Lord is leading His Church. This is what is emerging, and this is what is needed if we want to see revival and awakening. If we want to see this occur, it will entail pastors encouraging those under their care to join with believers from other congregations and demonstrate the love of God right in their own neighborhoods.

I talked with a pastor whose small groups had gone through *Neighborhood Initiative and the Love of God*, and he fully understands the implication of where it might take not only his church, but other churches in his city. Almost every church offers small groups, each by a different name. For example, small groups in my home church are called Mosaic. Another church refers to them as Life Groups. Still another calls them Connect Groups. But what if we just called them all Neighborhood Groups and joined them together right where people live? That would bring people attending different churches together in the same small group with others living in the same neighborhood. Wow! That would be radical. And that would also be reformation. The whole Church experiencing loving community together, so that those in our neighborhoods would know that we are Jesus' disciples. We would literally become the answer to Jesus' high priestly prayer:

> "My prayer is not for them alone. I pray also for those who will believe in me [that also includes us] through their message, that all of them may be one, Father, just as you are in me and I am in you. May they also be in us so that the world may believe that you have sent me. I have given them the glory that you gave me, that they may be one as we are one: I in them and you in me—so that they

may they be brought to complete unity. Then the world will know that you sent me and have loved them even as you have loved me." John 17:20–23 NIV

I firmly believe that this is what Jesus is up to in this particular season of Church history. He is answering His own prayer by making us one; the whole Church ministering in every neighborhood in every city. This is huge. This is reformation.

"Next to the Blessed Sacrament itself, your neighbor is the holiest object presented to your senses."

—C. S. Lewis, *The Weight of Glory*

SECTION 1

Moving Away from the Attractional Model

Chapter 1

Restoring Jesus' Intention for His Church

"Going Back to Our Roots"

*The Word became flesh and made his dwelling among us.
We have seen his glory, the glory of the one and only Son, who came
from the Father, full of grace and truth.*
—John 1:14 NIV

The definition of *radical* is "going back to the root" or relating to the *origin*. I believe it is the intent of the Lord to take us back to our roots, back to doing what He commanded the first disciples to do:

Then Jesus came to them [His disciples] and said, "All authority in heaven and on earth has been given to me. Therefore go and make disciples of all nations, baptizing them in the name of the Father and of the Son and of the Holy Spirit, and teaching them to obey everything I have commanded you. And surely I am with you always, to the very end of the age." (Matthew 28:18–20 NIV)

This command stands as Jesus' directive to His Church. Out of fear, a desire for comfort, or isolation, you name it, the American church has left the moorings of this command and has drifted away from what the Lord has called His Church to do in the world.

Attractional Model

The American church, for the most part, has as its operating system an attractional model. Very succinctly, I characterize the attractional church model in this way: We want people to come to our church. We are always looking for another way to attract people to our buildings, to hear our pastor, to participate in our programs. As defined by the attractional church, success is marked by increased attendance. But is this really success? Is this really what Jesus had in mind for His Church? Isn't this diametrically opposed to Jesus' command to "go" and make disciples? Moreover, might not this model of attracting members stand in opposition to the exponential growth model that Jesus set forth for His Church through the making and dispersing of disciples? The sad thing is that most of the addition in the American church today is through transfer growth. It is the growing of one church at the expense of another. In other words, we are cannibalizing ourselves.

Incarnational Model

The incarnational church is the church that models what Jesus did in His three years of ministry. As Dallas Willard so wisely pointed out, "One of the things we often miss is that His mission in the world is incarnational. It comes through people. Incarnation is not just a theological doctrine. It's a doctrine about how we live. And if we are going to bring Christ to our world, our cities, our neighbors, then we do it in our own person, skin on skin contact, face to face, relationships to others where we manifest a love that is beyond human possibilities and yet is within human actuality, because God makes it so."[3] Not only does the

Lord want this for individual believers, but He wants this for His Church collectively. He wants the Whole Church in every city to be given over completely to loving its neighbor as itself. He wants us to move back to the model that He established for His Church in the very beginning.

In countries where the church is persecuted, they follow Jesus' instructions. They have no other choice. Recently, I talked with Pastor Surya Mani Bhandari who has planted ten congregations in Nepal where Christian pastors lead the flock of God at the risk of losing their own lives. Pastor Bhandari was himself kidnapped, but eventually escaped. When he had the opportunity, he would secretly return to preach to his congregation and afterward would flee from those who were trying to track him down. He has presently gained political asylum here in the United States and regularly gathers with pastors to pray.

I asked Surya, "How does the church grow in the community where you pastored?" His answer intrigued me. He said people from the Christian community lovingly reach out to their neighbors. Once that neighbor comes to faith, they begin to meet with him regularly to pray for fifteen minutes, steadily increasing the amount of time they spend in prayer in the days and weeks to follow. In time, they ask him to reach out in love to his own neighbors, just as they did to him. Thus the church begins to grow quietly and organically through the neighborhoods.

As I was listening to Surya share this simple plan it reminded me of what Jesus told the 70 to do in Luke 10:5–9 (NIV):

"When you enter a house, first say, 'Peace to this house.' If someone who promotes peace is there, your peace will rest on them; if not, it will return to you. Stay there, eating and drinking whatever they give you, for the worker deserves his wages. Do not move around from house to house. When you enter a town and are welcomed, eat what is offered to you. Heal the sick who are there and tell them, 'The kingdom of God has come near to you.'"

A Story of Two Missionaries

As I was writing this book, I was invited to a memorial service for a dear friend of mine, Patricia Johnson, who served the Lord faithfully with the Jewish community here in Los Angeles. The pastor who was officiating at her service shared a story that captured my attention. He spoke of two missionaries who served at different times on the same island. Here's the story he shared:

> "A true-life story is told of a missionary who traveled to the South Pacific to share the good news of Jesus Christ with the local people on an island. Back in the day, missionaries knew that they would not come back to their families because of the mode of travel. When he arrived at the island, he did not initially open his Bible and preach to them. Instead he learned their customs, loved them, was humble, gentle, and forgave them when they did wrong. After two years of being there, he contracted a rare disease and died. A year later, another missionary came to that same island, but his approach was different. He opened the Bible and began to teach the people how God in heaven sent His Son, Jesus, to love people, die for their sins, and provide eternal life for all who believe. When they heard this, they said, 'We know that man! He came here to live with us, and then he died.' The missionary said, 'No, Jesus lived 2,000 years ago and died on a cross and resurrected for the forgiveness of our sins.'

> "*The islanders then responded, 'Then we want to accept Jesus Christ as our Lord and Savior right now and go to heaven when we die.'*"

Because of the incarnational approach taken by the first missionary, the islanders mistook the second missionary's account of Jesus as being that of their former friend. But then, upon realizing that this new missionary was speaking of Someone greater than their friend, they eagerly sought to become disciples of our Lord.

God is calling His Whole Church to live our lives in our neighborhoods just like that missionary, just as Jesus did, so that they might mistake us for Jesus and want to have what we have—a relationship with the heavenly Father. Won't you join Him in the work He is doing right outside your door?

CHAPTER 2

SEEING THE CHURCH WITH NEW EYES
"Getting Over Ourselves"

I am not a theorist, but a practitioner. I love the Lord's Church; I believe it has a promising future, because Jesus said it would. But because of what I see in the Scriptures, I believe there is a better way for the Church to operate than what we now experience, and I would call that better way the "Jesus model."

Having willingly set aside His divinity, Jesus modeled an incarnational life for His disciples to follow. As the ministry of the disciples grew, they modeled the same incarnational life to those who followed them. And when all the followers of Jesus live in this manner, it becomes *"the whole church taking the whole Gospel to the whole city one neighborhood at a time."* It becomes Jesus-followers from different congregations working together in every city to bring the love of God to every neighbor, whether that neighbor actually lives close by or is simply encountered naturally during the course of one's daily activities.

Many of us Christians here in the U.S. have great concerns about the state of our nation, but why is there seemingly no serious alarm or outcry among Christians about the condition of the church? "In America, 3,500–4,000 churches close their doors each year."[4] That amounts to over ten churches closing their doors each and every day (This figure doesn't account for new churches that are opening their doors every day). And if that isn't enough, "Churches lose an estimated 2,765,000 people each year to nominalism and secularism."[5] Shouldn't it concern us that the church in America is dying out? Shouldn't it concern us that we who are the salt and light of world are becoming irrelevant and marginalized right here in our own country?

There are those who are happy with the growth of their own local congregation even though the church in America is in major decline. Are we only concerned about our own congregation, or are we going to take into consideration the *Whole Church* and work together for the cause of Christ? We have for far too long isolated ourselves from one another. Jesus would be so pleased with His Church if it became the embodiment of what He prayed for in His High Priestly Prayer in John 17: "[May they] be brought to complete unity. Then the world will know that you sent me and have loved them even as you have loved me" (John 17:23 NIV).

The mark of true biblical success is the whole Church working together so that the world comes to know that God the Father sent His Son to earth. How are we doing with that? I am not asking how your congregation is doing. I am asking, "How is the *Whole Church* doing in each of our cities?" This is the mind-set and concern that pastors and leaders in cities should have. Are we all looking out for one another, or are we so busy that we don't have time for one another and the advance of God's kingdom in our cities? This is the very reason why the apostle Paul said to the Philippians, "Not looking to your own interests but each of you to the interests of the others" (Philippians 2:4 NIV). He was encouraging them to overcome any self-centeredness in the church in their city, knowing that it would only bring division and further hinder the flow of the Gospel in their city.

Dallas Willard addressed this profound divide among congregations in his book, *Living in Christ's Presence*:

> "Once you back up and look at it, it's obvious that the separation between the churches in our communities is one of the hardest things to get past to appreciate what Christ is doing in the world. I have tried to approach this by saying to ministers that the most important part of your ministry is that to other ministers. Come to know them, and begin to get over the idea of separation and competition.
>
> "Now, again this is for spokespersons for Christ. Of course, ministers are central to this in many ways, but it isn't just the ministers; it's all Christians. The church in a community is not one of the churches. There are groups we can call churches if we wish. I think this turns out to be very harmful, and you have to come to grips with usage and reality; it's hard to do anything about it, though people have tried to do that. They have given their church a different name—and usually they wind up being another denomination.
>
> "Individually we can do something. Individually we can know our fellow spokespersons, and we can make a point of making sure that there are some of them that are not like us. We can then begin to support them and pull for their success. Wanting other churches to succeed is one of the most important things we can do. Someone might say, well, but there's so-and-so, and give a name. But that doesn't matter. We are disciples or we are nothing. As disciples, we love one another, and we care for one another, and we recognize the situation that we are

in a local community. We claim one another. It may scare the others to death until they get used to it, and they will want to know what you are up to supporting them and pulling for them to succeed in God's terms. We can, I believe, make a start."[6]

I have worked in the trenches of local congregations for over forty years. I have served in small, medium, and large churches during those years. I also spent four years in a "house church." It is my hope and desire, for as long as I am able, to participate with the Lord and other leaders in moving local congregations forward in becoming one body that loves the *Whole Church* and its neighbors. As you might imagine, it hasn't always been easy. There have been times that it seemed impossible, but I am seeing in our day a movement toward a model that Jesus wants for His Church. It is an incarnational model, the Whole Church being the embodiment of Jesus in the world. That is, carrying on the work that Jesus did while He was here on earth, but now as one collective body in the world. With this kind of oneness, coupled with the empowering of the Holy Spirit, we will see revival in our churches and awakening in our cities.

CHAPTER 3

TAKE OFF THAT OLD GARMENT
"The Old Is Not Better!"

> He told them this parable: "No one tears a piece out of a new garment to patch an old one. Otherwise, they will have torn the new garment, and the patch from the new will not match the old. And no one pours new wine into old wineskins. Otherwise, the new wine will burst the skins; the wine will run out and the wineskins will be ruined. No, new wine must be poured into new wineskins. And no one after drinking old wine wants the new, for they say, 'The old is better.'"
> —Luke 5:36–39 NIV

Accepting the Whole New Garment

It seems to me that the meaning behind Jesus' parable of the patched garment and the new wineskins is this: the Gospel of the Kingdom, which He was proclaiming, could not be altered to fit into the Pharisees' paradigm or way of living. As noted in the Jamieson, Fausset, and Brown commentary, the Kingdom of God and the rituals of Jewish tradition do not co-exist "by a mongrel mixture of the ascetic ritualism of the old with the spiritual freedom of the new economy, both are disfigured and destroyed."[7]

It also seems to me that something is often overlooked when reading this parable. Jesus says, "No one tears a patch from a *new garment* and sews it on an old one." Often the focus is on the patch being sewn onto the old garment rather than on what is lost by not accepting the new garment just as it is. By utilizing the new garment only for the purpose of retaining the old, the remainder of the garment is rendered useless. It has been destroyed in the process of trying to maintain the old. Likewise, when the Lord brings something new to His Church, our tendency is to pick and choose what we want from the new thing He offers rather than accepting the whole new garment.

Years ago, I bought a beautiful, large, offset umbrella for our patio. I liked that umbrella a lot. Six people could sit comfortably under it around a table. As the years went by, the umbrella began to deteriorate. I continued to buy new parts for it and repaired it over and over. But as time went by, it became harder and harder to keep the old umbrella working properly. I repaired parts of the metal supports with tape. The crank didn't work any longer, so I had to push it up manually. Finally, one day I noticed that the center ring that held all of the metal supports was cracked. I was disheartened. The umbrella that had served me so well for so many years no longer served its purpose. I went out that day and purchased a brand new model. Once I began using the new umbrella, I found that I really didn't miss the old one. It functioned perfectly. I am not sure why I became so attached to that old umbrella, but I sure like the new one a lot better. Well, we can do the same with the attractional church model. It served us well for a season as God intended, but it might be time to put on the new garment that will serve the Church so much better as we move into the future.

A Time to Dismantle

Right now, as I am typing, there is a church facility next to ours that is being dismantled. They are literally demolishing every inch of it. The facility was well over fifty years old. They are replacing it with low-cost housing. It will be a beautiful new four-story structure that will provide for the needy in our community—not just housing, but real care for those who will live in the seventy-seven apartments.

I am sure there is a lot of emotion for those who were once a part of the congregation and met in the "sanctuary" and a sense of loss with all the memories that were shared with others during those years. I am sure there are those who are disheartened that yet another "church" is being removed from our community. But as I walked into our building one day after watching some of the demolition, I said to two of our staff members, "You can destroy a church, but you can't destroy *the* Church." It is *not* as the little kid's church rhyme asserts, "Here is the Church. Here is the steeple. Open the doors and see all the people." The Church *is* the people, the people of God. These are the precious ones that make up the Body of Christ, His body here on earth today.

As I put forward the suggestion that we consider dismantling the attractional church model, I am sure that some of you will share similar emotions with those who were watching their old church facility being demolished. Many of us have become quite accustomed to this particular operating system. There are so many memories wrapped up in the way we have always done church. Removing some of the programs could be very painful. Letting go of what is familiar and comfortable is never easy. However, if churches want to become the embodiment of Jesus in the world, then concessions need to be made to accommodate the new wine that Jesus is pouring out in our day.

The Tyranny of the *Or* and the Genius of the *And*

Most churches today are largely internally focused. They have a high emphasis on programs and small groups that are designed primarily to meet the needs of those in the church. Evaluate your own church and ask yourself, which activities are intended for those in your church and which ones are truly designed for those outside? Take a look at your bulletin or your website. You may be surprised to find that there are a few for those outside of the church, but primarily the focus is for those on the inside. As time has progressed from Jesus and Paul's day, we have become for the most part more of an exclusive club. I know there are exceptions, but local churches overall cater to the believer. This is the church that we have inherited, and our way of doing church has kept the Church from doing what Jesus did when He was here on earth.

When we first started Neighborhood Initiative (then called Mission Reseda), we targeted eight square blocks around our church facility to outwardly demonstrate the love of God to the surrounding community. At the time, we were partnering with the Los Angles Police Department, so when we would go door to door, we would let them know that we were from Valley Vineyard Church and that we were working in conjunction with the police department. But as we expressed what we were doing in their neighborhood, rarely did the residents know where our church facility was located. Though we were located on a prominent street, only blocks away, they had no recollection of our building. Today, many can identify our church building, but that is only because we have gone out into the local neighborhoods and engaged the local residents right where they live.

Becoming the incarnational church will require both pastors and members of their congregations to make different choices from those made in the past. If we are truly serious about intentionally loving our neighbors, then we will have to say no to certain internally focused activities, in order that we can give the needed time and attention to our neighbors. However, it is very important that we maintain a balance here. It is not either-or, but both-and. It is easy to overreact when you see the importance of loving your neighbor and throw the baby out with the bathwater.

In those early days of Neighborhood Initiative, our pastor asked if I would teach on a Sunday morning on the subject of loving our neighbors. My message was entitled, "Overcoming a Fortress Mentality." I started my message by showing a video clip from the movie *Sister Act*, which in a humorous way shows the transition of a church from being internally focused to being externally engaged. In the clip there is pushback from Reverend Mother, the one in charge, who is resistant to letting the sisters go out into the neighborhood. She felt it was unsafe to go out into the streets. She had become comfortable in doing church as usual. Even after the wonderful things that were going on in the neighborhood by the sisters, she resisted what they were doing. Reverend Mother is a perfect example of one who is attached to an "old garment." She could not accept the new things that were being poured out in the community. After watching the clip, one could easily become critical of being internally focused. However, I pointed out in the message the significance of the tyranny of the "or" and the genius of the "and."

In the best-selling book by Jim Collins and Jerry Porras titled *Built to Last*: Successful Habits of Visionary Companies, the authors introduced the concept that most companies live in the "tyranny of the or": either-or dichotomies that force the choice between profit and benefit to customers, between speed and quality, and so on. The authors point out that successful companies actually pursue two seemingly contrary goals simultaneously. For instance, Starbucks serves quality coffee that you can get in a drive-through. No one will question their success. I believe to be a "successful" church we should be inwardly focused *and* externally engaged. We should pursue these two seemingly contrary goals simultaneously.

CHAPTER 4

ESTABLISHING AUTHENTIC RELATIONSHIPS

"How Long Have You Been Coming to Church Here?"

It is important on the part of church leadership to prayerfully consider what is really necessary for equipping the saints in our churches to be a community that loves their neighbors as themselves. Acts 2:42–47 (NIV) is a good model to work off of if we want to evaluate what is really essential for church life.

> "They devoted themselves to the apostles' teaching and to fellowship, to the breaking of bread and to prayer. Everyone was filled with awe at the many wonders and signs performed by the apostles. All the believers were together and had everything in common. They sold property and possessions to give to anyone who had need. Every day they continued to meet together in the temple courts. They broke bread in their homes and ate together with glad and sincere hearts, praising God and enjoying the favor of all the people. And the Lord added to their number daily those who were being saved."

Sadly, the church in America has moved far away from this model that the Holy Spirit established in the early days of the Church. We have stifled or replaced this model with our many meetings and programs that, for the most part, keep us so busy that we don't establish authentic relationships among believers in the local church and, maybe more importantly, keep us out of touch with those outside the church who are desperately in need of establishing such relationships. As I interpret the model reflected in the book of Acts, there are four things that are really essential for church life:

1. **The gathering of the saints** to worship God and the teaching of the Word.
2. **Discipleship** for spiritual, personal, and leadership development.
3. **The church that meets geographically in homes for community life** where we care for one another (includes sharing of our possessions), develop meaningful relationships with one another, pray together, minister the gifts of the Spirit, integrate the teaching of the Word of God into our daily lives, gather for meals together with genuineness and laughter, and stimulate one another to love our neighbors as ourselves.
4. **The love of neighbor**, which includes those in our own household, our actual neighbors, those whom we naturally come into contact with each day, and any missional work in our city or elsewhere.

These four essentials should never be squeezed out of church life. When we fill our church calendars with a host of activities that replace these four essentials, we move away from being the Church that Jesus had in mind and that the apostles modeled for future generations.

Am I saying that all of those programs and meetings in our churches should not exist? No! I am asking, "What is really necessary beyond the four essentials?" Here are some questions to help you evaluate what is really needed in your church.

- What program, if dropped, would cause serious problems to the move of God's Spirit in your church?
- Is a specific program really meeting an important need in the life of your congregation or the community?
- Has a program run its course, and has it been put on life support to try to keep it alive?
- Do people from your church attend a particular program out of obligation or habit, rather than participating because it is life-giving and important?
- Is there a real sense that God is in the program and everyone involved is excited to participate?
- Is a program or meeting such a "sacred cow" that no one is willing to say, "We should stop it?" Sacred cow programs are easy to spot. Attendance has dropped off and a few holdouts continue to attend out of obligation because "that's the way we've always done it."
- Is a program or a variety of programs making it impossible to give priority time to the four essentials mentioned above?

Over my years in church leadership, I have observed that new people enter into church life very excited about the many opportunities that are available to them. Initially, they may get their feet wet by participating in some or even several of the programs, but eventually they settle down into attending church services and maybe one or two other events. Generally, they will not participate in more than one weekly evening event (I know there are exceptions). It is nice that the church offers this smorgasbord of activities for everyone, but is this the local church's purpose? Are we meant to keep our members busy, or are we to go into the world and make disciples? Here's an idea: why don't we offer some of our good programs to people outside of our churches? How about Vacation Bible School *in the neighborhood*, not at the church? How about a Christmas tea for the women on your block? How about a movie night in your backyard for children in your neighborhood? How about a chili cook-off for all the neighbors? The possibilities are limitless! I know some are uncomfortable about what I am suggesting. However, there are those who would find this refreshing. They would love to be a part of a church that is making a difference not only in the lives of believers, but also in the lives of those in their community. If this is the case for you, then you should find this most helpful.

CHAPTER 5

LET'S STOP BEING "CHURCHY"
"My Pathetic Story!"

When I was a fairly new believer, I attended a student orientation gathering at a Christian college where one of the students mentioned that all of his friends were Christians. I remember thinking, "I only have a few Christian friends." At the time, it was hard for me to imagine only having Christian friends. However, as I became more involved in the local church and pastoring, I became more removed from people outside of the church. Eventually, I could say, like that student, "All of my friends are Christians."

I graduated from a local Bible college and seminary, and for most of the time while I was in school I was the college pastor of a thriving college ministry. During those years the group grew from about thirty-five to around 500 on Sunday mornings. We had ministries on different local campuses. God was really moving in the lives of the students and those who participated in the college group.

After ten years of pastoral ministry, the Lord called me away from a paid position as a pastor to work for an advertising firm while pastoring a house church. Initially, I worked on a folding machine, but eventually I moved on to building community bulletin boards and installing them on market walls. I loved the job, and I loved that season of my life. I traveled all over California and was able, from time to time, to bring my boys along with me on the job. Of course, when I was on the coast, I would find time to surf some of the local surf spots.

When I first started the job in the warehouse, I was intimidated by those who worked at the company, especially those in the front office. I felt very awkward, like a fish out of water. I had spent ten years away from un-churched people, and I couldn't relate to them anymore. I realized that my schooling and church-life experience really didn't prepare me for being with people outside the church. I found myself tagging alongside the only Christian in the warehouse. He had a goofy sense of humor, which I enjoyed. He made me feel safe. As I reflect on it today, I was pretty pathetic. I was so far from being like Jesus in the world. This experience opened my eyes to how "churchy" I had become and made me realize that pastoral leadership really didn't prepare me to relate naturally and authentically with those outside of the Church. I often wonder why pastors are trained, for the most part, by professors who have not been pastors and people in the church are taught by pastors who are not really in the world.

After eight years of working for this national company, I really connected with many of the people and I shared the Lord when He gave me the opportunity. Just before I left the company I was honored with "Employee of the Month." The honor itself wasn't so much of a big deal, but what it represented to me *was* a big deal. It was a message from the Lord to me that I graduated from being "churchy" to being a "real person" again; one who could relate to those outside the church. It was more significant than my degrees and my accomplishments in church ministry, because I became "Jesus with skin on." This is what compels me now, to help those in the church to be like Jesus in the world.

Becoming an incarnational person really doesn't require higher education. Most of Jesus' disciples were "uneducated." It doesn't require another conference or program. It requires being immersed in the lives of those in our community and neighborhoods, just as I became immersed in the lives of those I worked with on the job.

CHAPTER 6

LET'S MOVE TOWARD BEING "HOME CENTERED"
"Our Building Shouldn't Sit Empty!"

It is hard to imagine not using our building as often as possible. We have invested so much time and money in it. It shouldn't sit empty. With this mind-set we have made it our objective to fill our buildings up all week long with activities primarily focused on the church family. The more activities at the building, the more pleased we are with our church. We pride ourselves when our church parking lot is filled night after night. The sad thing is that "church-life" is then primarily reserved for the building. When the church facility becomes the center for all of our church activity, it sucks us out of our communities and out of our neighborhoods. It separates us from the very people that Jesus sent us out to love.

Most people in churches today are so busy at the building with programs and/or meetings that the very thought of doing something in their homes or neighborhoods is out of the question. Just the *thought* of doing another thing exhausts most people in the church today, especially the parents of active children. If the church is going to live as Jesus did in the world, then we are going to have to reassess our priorities. We are going to have to ask ourselves, "What is really important?" This is a very significant question. Often we go through the motions of church-life without asking this important question. If we are going to take the Great Commission ("Go and make disciples") and the Great Commandment ("Love God and love our neighbor") more seriously, then we simply must reconsider how and where we spend our time.

When I say these things I don't share them in a vacuum. When I was an associate pastor, I had to ask myself the very same question: "What is really important?" As I honestly answered this question, I began to say no to certain church activities so that I could give time to the things that had greater priority. Those things fall into the four essentials mentioned earlier. I know some of these programs and meetings are really good things to do, but keep in mind, *good is often the enemy of the best.* You may have to walk away from things that are "good" in order to spend more time with your family, in a neighborhood group, or with your neighbors.

At the time of this writing, I am teaching two of my neighbors out of the book of James. One of them had never read the Bible in English before. He absolutely loves it, and God is speaking to him when we gather together at Starbucks. He recently invited another neighbor and myself to join him at his house for dinner. And both the relationship and the conversation continue to grow. This is discipleship-making at its most basic level, and it has become my top priority. More importantly, we see that it was a top priority for Jesus as well.

When Jesus entered the city of Jericho, He spotted Zacchaeus in a tree and said, "I am coming to your house today." In so doing, Jesus modeled for His disciples the importance of one-on-one, relational ministry. He obviously saw in Zacchaeus a "person of peace," one who would be receptive to His teaching. Therefore, He purposely took the time to break bread with Zacchaeus and forge a relationship. The results were astounding (Luke 19:1–10).

Isn't this the type of relationship building the Lord would have us do right where we live and work? Following Jesus' lead, shouldn't we be looking for our own Zacchaeus-like relationships in our own neighborhoods?

There are many contexts through which the Gospel will spread; however, in Jesus' directive to His disciples, the context for the advance of God's Kingdom was through the home. He instructed them to go to a town or village and find a "worthy person" or a "person of peace" and stay at that person's house (Matthew 10:11–14). We see then that the home was envisioned as the center for ministry, the point from which the Gospel message would begin to spread from one neighborhood to the next.

At the very inception of the Church, disciples fellowshipped together, and "broke bread in their homes" (Acts 2:46, NIV). They also gathered at the temple, but by gathering in people's homes, they moved outside of their close-knit community and began to engage with others who lived close by. The result was that they enjoyed the favor of *all the people* and the Lord added to their numbers day by day (Acts 2:47).

Have you ever wondered why the modern Church doesn't look like the early Church, the one recorded for us in the book of Acts? One might respond by saying that life was simpler then; that the world has become more complex now, and that the Church is more sophisticated with its facilities and programs.

But is that the true answer? Have we slowed in making disciples because we have gotten more sophisticated, or has the playing field changed?

Maybe one of the reasons the Church doesn't grow as it once did is because neither the home nor the neighborhood is at the center of ministry activity. Everything takes place in a building of our making, not in the location where we were first directed.

Thus, we stagnate in place, trying to get others to come to us rather than plant seeds of the Kingdom where we were told.

The plan was so simple: go from house to house, spreading news of God's Kingdom, and making disciples. By adhering to the plan, the Church would easily reproduce, and the good news would spread. But, deviate from the plan, and the Church becomes impotent, unable to effectively reproduce.

For the record, I am not opposed to church buildings and facilities. They can become wonderful places for worship and training. But the primary place to develop relationships that will allow us to lead someone toward the Kingdom is not the church . . . it is the home. Our home is a place where, hopefully, our neighbors can feel comfortable, where they can speak freely and explore their faith. Going to church might be threatening, but breaking bread from house-to-house is anything but intimidating.

Maybe it's time to get back to the original plan, to look for that person of peace and meet them right where they live. Maybe it's time to re-think our approach of getting them to worship with us on Sunday morning versus just learning how God has been at work in their lives.

CHAPTER 7

DONES AND NONES

"I Am Done with Church!"
"I Never Wanted to Go There Anyway!"

At a Neighborhood Collective gathering in Longmont, Colorado, in February 2016, church leaders engaged in neighboring ministry from across the country listened intently as Dr. Josh Packard, the author of *Church Refugees*, shared some very disturbing trends. His research revealed that 30.5 million people have left the church in America, and that another 7.5 million are on the verge of leaving.

Packard has labeled those who have left as the "Dones." They are people who are done with the church as an organization and institution, but (and this is a very important distinctive) not done with God or their faith. He pointed out they were explicit and intentional about opting out of the institutional church. They did not drift away. They left purposefully.

Packard was able to identify several things that the Dones wanted from their church experience but were unable to find:

- Activity, not bureaucracy
- Conversation, not doctrine
- A community of authenticity, not culture of judgment
- Meaningful ministry, not moral prescriptions

What surprises me concerning Packard's findings is his conclusion that neighboring is the answer for those who left the church, that the Dones will re-engage through neighborhood ministry. I agree with him. The Church wants to woo them back into their buildings, but neighboring takes us out where they live, allowing us to become bridge builders. Instead of them having to come back into the church building, to sit where they don't want to sit and to participate in something that has not been life giving, they can experience the flow of love from brothers and sisters right where they live.

What I share, I share from experience. For four years I was a Done. I had no desire to sit in a pew or participate in an institutional church again. It was by the grace of God that I entered back into the life of a church. Some dear friends helped me at a time when I was really hurting, and it was through those dear friends that the Lord spoke to me and led me back into a fellowship with some loving believers. It helped that they were meeting at a junior high school. It didn't feel like "church." These people were beautiful and accepted me and loved me right where I was at.

However, there are Dones out there who are not hurting and have not walked away from the Lord, but are serving the Lord and are quite fruitful. By entering into neighborhood ministry, we can join with many of our Done brothers and sisters, locking arms and serving together right where we both live. For those who are out there and are hurting, like I was, we can come alongside of them, care for them, and encourage them to re-engage with their churched brethren in the Lord's work.

There is another group of people that Packard refers to in his book. He calls them the Nones. These are people who do not believe in God and would never set foot in a church or any other religious institution. These are those who can't imagine why anyone would ever go to church. Many view Christians with disdain and have categorized us as judgmental, out of touch with the real world. They feel that culture has progressed and that Christians, for the most part, have nothing to offer them or society. Many would be happy if Christians didn't exist.

Then how are the Nones to be reached? Again, Josh Packard believes neighboring is the answer. Surprisingly, it is precisely because they view Christians as judgmental that we might be afforded our best opportunity to reach the Nones. If we genuinely love our neighbors as ourselves, we can break through their preconceived notions of Christians, thereby leading them to a place where they can truly encounter the love of God. In essence, Packard affirms what Jesus said: "Let your light shine before men, that they may see your *good* deeds and praise your Father in heaven" (Matthew 5:16). The Greek word Jesus uses here for "good" is *kalos*. The word means "beautiful," and beautiful works are those that turn the attention of others toward our Father in heaven. If we demonstrate beautiful works in our neighborhoods, hopefully, those who would never step a foot in a church may turn their attention heavenward.

Why are there so many Dones and Nones?

Shahkrokh "Shah" Afshar is a dear friend of mine. Born in Iran, raised Muslim, today he is a devoted Christian and has led many Muslims to the Lord. He founded and pastored the first Iranian Christian organization in the United States. Shah has been instrumental in reaching the Muslim world with the Gospel. His work as a professor and as a Muslim world mission coordinator for Foursquare Missions International expanded his influence worldwide. Though his influence is worldwide, he believes the best way to reach Muslims is through loving your neighbor.

Shah is an original. He shares unique insights with humor and wit. As he openly admits, he can be unfiltered. I believe Shah has captured the great need for neighboring when it comes to the Dones and Nones. Here's his story in his own words.

Shah Afshar's Story

As I came out of the bookstore, I had one thought in mind, "I wish I was dead!" The thought of death was the most soothing thought I had had since I'd started college.

The year was 1971, and after two semesters of college, it was obvious that getting a degree in civil engineering, something that had brought me to the U.S., was not going to be that easy.

In two semesters, I'd gotten nothing but lousy grades, which had made me quite ashamed of being the failure that I'd become. But even more painful was letting my parents down, who had made a great sacrifice to get their oldest to America. So, not being able to live up to a standard that my Iranian culture had set for me, my next step was committing suicide. But that day, as I came out of the school's bookstore, something happened that gave me a glimmer of hope.

As I stepped out the door, with the weight of the whole world on my shoulders and my head bowed down, the guy coming toward me was dancing and scat singing. As he got next to me, he looked me in the eyes and asked, "How are you?"

Never being one who hides his emotions, but at the same time not expecting anything, I said, "I'm not doing well."

What happened next, as simple as it might sound to some of my readers, was something that I'll never forget for the rest of my life.

The man stopped dead in his tracks and asked, "Is there anything I can do for you?" A stranger, a man I didn't know, stopped and offered to help me. I needed that so much. I deeply wanted to know that someone cared about this worthless failure of a man.

I don't remember what happened next. I might have said, "No, thanks!" and gone on my way. But I still remember that act of kindness and try to implement it in my Christian walk whenever I can.

I remember in one instance in particular, I was invited to fill in for my friend who is an adjunct professor at a Bible college. As it is my habit, I show up early. Because it was lunchtime, I sit on the retaining wall next to the entrance to the refectory. (Whatever happened to the dining hall?) I want to see how the students react toward a stranger who is much older than they are and seems not to belong to their school.

As these Bible college students, our future Christian leaders, begin to pass by me, I stare at them in hope that, out of respect for an elder, they would greet me, and at least be smiling at me, acknowledge me as a man who is made in the image of the God that they would be studying right after lunch.

Out of about 100 students who pass me by, only a few of them acknowledge my being and give me a hurried glance. That breaks my heart. Don't they realize that I might desperately be in need of a smile, a "how are you?" an affirmation that I am still a human being made in the image of God?

A day doesn't go by that I don't come across an article about the "Dones" and the "Nones," lamenting the fact that church attendance is drastically dropping in the U.S.

Many of these articles sound like Chicken Little running around and screaming, "The sky is falling! The sky is falling.

People are leaving the church. What can we do to bring them back? Maybe if the church offers better programs, then people will stay and the 'Dones' will come back and the 'Nones' will be attracted to the church again." But very few talk about why these people have left and why the Millennials are not going to church.

The issue isn't having better programs. The issue isn't having strobe lights and fog machines or having the music so loud that you need to hand out earplugs to the parishioners as they enter the sanctuary on Sunday mornings. I personally have no problem with any of that. But that will not solve some of the much deeper issues the church needs to face and resolve.

To think that better programs will solve the crisis the Church is facing is like the old joke about a man who had three ugly daughters. One day as he's walking on the beach, the man comes across a bottle, and when he opens it a genie pops out.

"For freeing me from this prison, I'll grant you a wish. What is it that you want?" said the genie.

Showing the genie a map, the man said, "I love Hawaii, but it's quite expensive to travel there several times a year. I want a bridge over the ocean that will directly connect L.A. to Hawaii."

The genie looked at the map and said, "I'm just a genie, not God. What you're asking is out of my hands. Is there anything else I can do for you?"

"Yes! I wish for my daughters to be married. Can you find them husbands?" pleaded the man.

"Do you have a picture of them?"

So, the man excitedly pulled a photo out of his wallet and showed it to the genie. Upon looking at it, the genie said, "Let me see the map again!"

There's a broken bridge between the church and the people. Until we rebuild that bridge; until we learn to smile at the old man sitting on the retaining wall rather than being too busy parsing Hebrew and Greek words for our next Sunday sermon, until we learn our neighbor's name who's lived next to us for several years, until we acknowledge the fact that we're all made in the image of God and should be treated as such, and until the church learns to love for no reason, but to obey Christ's commandment, the church will continue to be as unattractive as the man with the three daughters.[8]

CHAPTER 8

LET'S TAKE OFF THE BUSINESS SUIT
"Who's the Boss Anyway?"

> I have a special concern for you church leaders. I know what it's like to be a leader, in on Christ's sufferings as well as the coming glory. Here's my concern: that you care for God's flock with all the diligence of a shepherd. Not because you have to, but because you want to please God. Not calculating what you can get out of it, but acting spontaneously. Not bossily telling others what to do, but tenderly showing them the way. When God, who is the best shepherd of all, comes out in the open with his rule, he'll see that you've done it right and commend you lavishly.
> —1 Peter 5:1–4 (MSG)

For three years, the apostle Peter closely watched the life and ministry of Jesus. As he penned this portion of the Scriptures, I can't help but think that he reflected on the way that Jesus related to him, the other disciples, and the people around Him. Even though He had every right to use His authority as God to dictate what His disciples should do, Jesus chose to relate to them in the same way that Peter here instructs us as leaders. Dallas Willard pointed out in *The Spirit of the Disciplines*, "In 1 Peter those older in The Way are told to take the oversight of the flock of God, not by being forced to do so and not as lords over God's heritage, but as examples to the flock (5:2–3). The younger are then told to submit themselves to this gentle oversight by the elders, and all are caught up together as a community of mutual submission: 'Yea, all of you be subject one to another, and be clothed with humility: for God resisteth the proud and giveth grace to the humble'" (5:5 KJV) [9]

A "Boss" vs. a "Servant-Leader"

Which do you prefer, a leader who tells you what to do or one who tenderly shows you the way to do it? How do you respond to a controlling and intimidating leader? None of us likes an overbearing individual. We all respond much better to a leader who is *humble and gentle*. Remind you of anyone? Jesus said, "Take my yoke upon you and learn from me, for I am gentle and humble in heart, and you will find rest for your souls. For my yoke is easy and my burden is light" (Matthew 11:29–30 NIV). This is Jesus' only autobiographical statement about Himself. This is the type of leader that Jesus wants for His Church, one who provides an easy yoke for others; one who is truly a servant-leader as opposed to a top-down leader; one who is with you to show you how and not one who barks out orders. As Jesus said, "You know that the rulers of the Gentiles lord it over them, and their high officials exercise authority over them. Not so with you. Instead, whoever desires to become great among you, let him be your servant." (Matthew 20:25–26 NIV).

Sadly, churches today all too often lend themselves to the "lord it over them" type of leadership. I am not saying by any means that all leaders in the church today model this type of leadership. However, it is hard not to gravitate toward this style, especially if one is leading a very large congregation. There is a tendency to pull away from the people, to shepherd less, to attend countless staff meetings, and to spend endless hours cooped up in an office disconnected from others, all of which is more characteristic of the corporate world. How unfortunate that these leaders generally don't have time to relate to their flock. Yet Jesus modeled being with "the people." Throughout the Gospels, we see Him associating with the lowly, the disabled, women and children, tax gathers, and sinners. Isn't it interesting that He demonstrated an aversion to the authoritative leadership modeled by the religious leaders of His day?

I love John 1:14: "The Word became flesh and made his dwelling among us." Or as *The Message* puts it, "The Word became flesh and blood, and moved into the neighborhood."

Jesus took off His kingly garments and left heaven to associate with everyone. He did not become a part of a pecking order as the religious leaders of His day. He came not to be served, but to serve, and ultimately to give His life as a ransom for all of us. I love our Leader, and I love His style of leadership, for this is precisely the type of leadership that adds value and dignity to all those who choose to follow Him.

Now and then you come across a leader of a very large congregation that models Jesus' style of leadership. My hat goes off to this rare breed. From what I have observed, Chuck Swindoll is one of those unique individuals. I deeply respect him and have greatly benefited from his writings and teachings throughout the years.

I will never forget the time I stopped by Pastor Chuck's church to visit a good friend of mine. I had just installed a bulletin board in a nearby market and I was wearing my typical work clothes: jeans, T-shirt, and tennis shoes. In the process of visiting my friend, I encountered Pastor Chuck who then warmly invited me into his office, shut the door behind us, directed me to have a seat, and asked me for counsel. Can you imagine how surprised I was that this prominent pastor was seeking counsel from *me*? This moment spoke more highly to me about who he was as a brother in Christ than all of his writings and messages. As I reflect on that short little encounter many years ago, I am reminded that this is what servant-leaders are like. They see beyond position or even one's dress and place value in the person. May his tribe grow.

"CEO Model" vs. "The Body of Christ"

Recently, I had a conversation with a dear friend of mine who has given his life's blood to serving in the church. He has a passion to see the Body of Christ unified and loves to bring pastors together. He is on different boards of Christian organizations that foster oneness among churches and cares deeply for the homeless and underprivileged. He called me one day and asked, "Do you have some time to talk?" I said, "Sure!" He said that he had a revelation after inviting a local pastor to a gathering of other pastors in the area. The pastor responded by saying that he didn't have time to get together with other leaders. As he reflected on why the pastor responded this way, the light went on. He said, "The CEO model for churches does not allow pastors the time to get together." He continued by saying, "Our present model of church leadership doesn't unite, it separates."

I had never thought of referring to the present-day leadership model of churches as a CEO Model, but the more I thought about what my friend was saying, I began to see the similarities between organizational structures in the business world and those practiced within the Body of Christ. I also began to see how our model not only serves to separate pastors and congregations from one another, but it also flies in the face of what Jesus modeled for

His disciples. When pastors see themselves as CEOs or as bosses of a church staff, then their methods are contrary to both Peter's instruction and the kind of leadership style that Jesus exhibited.

In a CEO model, the one in charge is concerned first and foremost with measurable gains or improvements. Performance is everything, and rolling out the best product to the public is the top priority. And of course, people are expendable and can easily be replaced.

This may be business as usual in the corporate world, but not so in the Body of Christ. According to the apostle Paul, every member of Christ's Body is important and adds value. Dallas Willard and Gary Black, co-authors of *Divine Conspiracy Continued*, put it this way, "The local church is not a business, despite those who might treat it as such or wish it so. Various efficiency and effectiveness standards simply do not apply in many ministry situations. The soul is not like the body in its ability to heal. And the relational and sociological dynamics of the local church do not work the same as those of a corporation, a factory, or a government agency. Although there is much wisdom in the ways businesses and non-profit organizations work that the local church can and should learn from, applying identical expectations and standards is inappropriate in many situations and circumstances."[10]

Former U.S. Senate chaplain Richard Halverson's assessment of church may shed some light on the CEO model that we have inherited: "The church began as a fellowship of men and women centered on Jesus Christ. It went to Greece and became a philosophy. It went to Rome and became an institution. It went to Europe and became a culture. It came to America and became an enterprise."[11]

An unfortunate side effect of the CEO model is that churches too often view themselves as being in competition with one another, rather than working together for the common good and for a common purpose. The business of our own church will take precedence over our interaction with others. We become too busy working with our own "business" to have time for other pastors in the city. Connection with others in the Body of Christ is just not a priority. But if we value unity in the Body of Christ, should we not set aside our concerns over the business of our individual churches, striving instead for the Kingdom of God in our midst?

CHAPTER 9

CAPTIVATED WITH THE UNITY
"Why Can't We Obey the Scriptures?"

For years, I have had a passion for the oneness of Christ's body and have worked together with pastors in our city. I didn't always have this perspective. I was initially critical of those who held different beliefs or traditions than my own, but since the early '80s, my thinking has transformed, and I have grown to love and appreciate the *whole* Church, not just my small piece of it.

It was during the early '80s that I became captivated with Ephesians 4:1–3 (NIV) where Paul says:

> "As a prisoner for the Lord, then, I urge you to live a life worthy of the calling you have received. Be completely *humble* and *gentle*; be patient, bearing with one another in love. Make every effort to keep the unity of the Spirit through the bond of peace."

There are those words again . . . humble and gentle . . . the character of Jesus. Then I focused on the phrase "keep the unity of the Spirit." Paul says we are to make "every effort" to do this, even to the point of sweating over it (my paraphrase). Eugene Peterson in *The Message* renders this, ". . . but steadily, pouring yourselves out for each other in acts of love, alert at noticing differences and quick at mending fences." It took a while, but I finally came to realize that the unity of the Spirit is something we *already* have in the Body of Christ and that all we have to do is maintain it.

I was quite excited about this new revelation and began to pursue unity with others in the Body of Christ. It was during this time that I was invited out to lunch by Robert Fife, an adjunct professor of religion at UCLA, a wise and seasoned veteran of the faith. While at lunch, I shared with him my excitement about unity. He joined me in my enthusiasm, but he asked, "Did you know there are two unities mentioned in Ephesians 4?" I said, "No." He said, "The first one is in verse 3, the one you mentioned, and the second one is in verse 13 (NIV)." He quoted the second one to me: "Until we all reach unity in the faith and in the knowledge of the Son of God and become mature, attaining to the whole measure of the fullness of Christ." He said, "The first one we already attained, but the second one we need to work toward." I was fascinated by these two different unities and what he had to say. He said, "Imagine a room. Over the door is a sign that reads 'Unity of the Spirit,' and we all go inside and together we work toward the 'unity in the faith and in the knowledge of the Son of God.' However, what those in the church have done today is put 'unity in the faith and in the knowledge of the Son of God' at the door and say, 'We can't have unity of the Spirit until we agree with each other about our doctrine.'" That is, if we don't agree on what we believe about the minor nuances of the Scriptures then we can't have unity of the Spirit.

I came away from that conversation with a greater appreciation for the Whole Church, and today can say, "I love the Church of Jesus Christ in its entirety." I desire to work together toward the unity of the faith, not through debate or argument, but through humble and gentle discussion, letting the Holy Spirit reveal truth to me through others.

Over the years, I have observed that there is a growing unity among pastors. Walls seem to be coming down in cities all over our country. It is an exciting day to be alive, even if the church in America is in decline. There is quite a cross-section of pastors meeting for prayer and joining forces to serve in their community. In *Neighborhood Initiative and the Love of God*, I mentioned that pastors in the San Fernando Valley of Los Angeles began praying together in January 2001. We set the following as our vision: to pray together, to build relationships with one another, and to wait on the Lord to show us His plan for winning our city. In 2011, it became apparent that Neighborhood Initiative had become that plan. Through our united prayer, His intention had become quite clear. His purpose was to bring people together from a variety of churches in order to demonstrate the love of God to all our neighbors. Thus our common purpose has become "the Whole Church taking the whole Gospel to the whole city one neighborhood at a time."

Having this common purpose has served to draw us together much closer than we were before. I am reminded of what Paul said to the brethren at Philippi:

> "If you have any encouragement from being united with Christ, if any comfort from his love, if any common sharing in the Spirit, if any tenderness and compassion, then make my joy complete by being like-minded, having the same love, *being one in spirit and of one mind.*" (Philippians 2:2, NIV; italics added for emphasis)

Without a common purpose or vision, pastors lose interest in gathering for prayer. But when they agree on a common purpose, all will pull together. There is a greater sense of oneness and anticipation of what can be done. Having a purpose or not having a purpose is like pushing or pulling several pieces of strings. If you try to push several at the same time they all go in different directions, but if they are all pulled in the same direction they all come together. I use this illustration of the string to point out an important truth: Oneness comes indirectly. If you try to pursue oneness among pastors simply for the sake of oneness alone, it more than likely will not happen. But if you put before them something of common interest such as bringing Christ's love to an entire city, they will rise to the occasion with people in their congregation.

CHAPTER 10

LET'S PLAY AS A TEAM
"Hey, Pass the Ball!"

I have been a Los Angeles Lakers fan for as long as I can remember. It is not in me to root for the Clippers, even if they have a better team. After the Lakers picked up All-Stars Dwight Howard and Steve Nash prior to the start of the 2012–13 NBA season, I never imagined that they would be fighting to get into the finals at the end of the season. With all those All-Stars, I thought that they would be near the top of the standings. I realize that they were all older players, but Kobe Bryant was still an amazing basketball player, scoring like he did when he was much younger. Oh how I loved watching Kobe's athleticism! God had given him a talent that is exciting to watch. So why couldn't the Lakers win?

One of the liabilities of being extremely talented is thinking that the team needs you in order to win. As he had gotten older, Kobe had adjusted his game and tried to become a facilitator (assisting others in getting the ball to the hoop). The Lakers game was much improved when he did this. The opposing team was not sure if the assist was going to come from Kobe or Steve Nash. However, when the going got tough, Kobe tended to default to what came very naturally to him. He would shoot the ball and try to win the game by himself. Sometimes this would work, and sometimes it wouldn't. On those occasions when Kobe took control, I noticed that his teammates were more reluctant to shoot.

They would just feed the ball to him. Thus the spirit of the team would become quenched, and Kobe's teammates would just let him play "his" game.

Like Kobe Bryant, some talented pastors who are gifted spiritually and have great prominence in their congregation, often find it hard to share their responsibilities with others. But when pastors push the ministry out to others and loosen the reins of their ministry, not only can God do mighty things, but the whole team wins.

There is nothing like watching a fluid basketball team working together as a team. Magic Johnson was a master at making this happen. In Los Angeles, we called it "Showtime." It was wonderful to watch. The opposing team didn't know what to expect and the crowds would roar watching the Lakers work as a single unit to accomplish something an individual could never accomplish by himself.

Decentralizing Out of Necessity

When I first started in college ministry, I literally did not know what I was doing. I didn't know the Word that well. I hadn't taught the Scriptures much to speak of, and if someone asked me a question I would often throw the question out to the rest of the class or I would let the person know I would get back to them the following week. Believe me, I didn't have Kobe's problem. From the get go, I needed every man, woman, and child to help me. I reached out to every person I could to help me in the ministry. The need for others actually proved to be my greatest asset in ministry. The "college group," as we called it back then, became an amazing team. The ministry grew and grew and grew. Before long, I had no idea how vast the ministry was and what everyone was doing. I know that sounds like I was being irresponsible, but many to this day would say that we were in the midst of a revival. I believe the Lord loves it when we turn our ministry over to His Spirit and let it grow through His orchestration.

Intentionally Decentralizing a Local Congregation

A few years back, I was invited by a good friend of mine, Gus Gill, to go to Denver and share with pastors there what we were doing in the San Fernando Valley with neighboring. My wife and I stayed in his home and had the opportunity to celebrate my friend's spiritual birthday, play some (lots!) poker, and attend their church. Gus had been a part of the college group I had pastored back in the '70s. Since then, he has served as a college chaplain, received his doctorate, and is now a pastor of a thriving congregation in Golden Colorado. He is highly committed to decentralizing the ministry. Like me, Gus is a real basketball enthusiast and appreciates the significance of working as a team. The pulpit on Sunday mornings is filled by various people from his staff. Small group discipleship is alive in their congregation, and the Lord is adding young people to their numbers. But what I noticed most was that my friend was really enjoying life. There were a lot of laughs and excitement about what the Lord was doing. The congregation wasn't dependent on him alone, because they were working together as a team. When his church board meets, they meet at Starbucks. You really couldn't see a demarcation between church activity and everyday life. His staff was made up of friends that liked to hang out together and take trips together. They weren't a part of a business, but a family. They were in each other's homes and others wanted to be a part of this family.

All too often, churches are centered around abilities and giftings of a single individual. The pastor becomes the congregation's focal point rather than the person by whom responsibilities and service is spread throughout the entire flock. It was so refreshing to be with Gus and to observe what God was doing in his church where everyone shares in the ministry.

The Whole Church Is a Team Sport

Perhaps Kobe Bryant's greatest asset is also his greatest liability; his inability to be a total team player. When one plays the game as well as he does, it is hard to be overly critical, but if he fails to use considerable talents to bring out the best in everyone else, then he might actually be standing in the way of the team's success. It is a conundrum. How can one play so well and yet at the same time contribute to the lack of success? But then, can't the same be said of certain pastors? Might there be those shepherds who are so good at what they do, yet success always seems just out of reach? Have we placed too much importance on one "player" but have missed the importance of the entire team playing together? A good basketball team seeks the involvement of the entire team, but when one player feels that winning depends on him alone, the rest of the team atrophies, not playing to their full potential. However, when a team works together as one unit, everyone begins reaching their potential, and players begin to augment each other rather than strive for individual gain. Watching a team work as one is a beautiful thing to observe. There is mutual encouragement and a desire to see one another succeed. That's the way one succeeds in basketball. Could it be that the same could be said for our congregations?

LET'S PLAY AS A TEAM

During the eightieth game of the 2012–13 NBA season, with only two games left in the regular season, Kobe Bryant tore his Achilles tendon. Due to the severity of the injury, he was unable to return to the team, and the Lakers were forced to play the last two games of the regular season without him. And yet, they were able to knock off two outstanding opponents and went into the finals as a seventh seed. Without their star player, everyone else on the team stepped up his game. There was no single star. They played as a team. For me, they were the two best games of the season. Everyone was pulling together to win.

I may have a fascination with watching individual athletes who perform at a high level, but I would much rather watch a team work together as a single unit to do something that not one of its members could accomplish alone. This is the way I see the Whole Church in a city. There is no way that one church alone can reach the whole city with the love of God. It takes the Whole Church working together as a single unit to do something that no one congregation can do by itself.

In the words of one pastor I know, this need for others is part of "God's design." In his view, there is a uniqueness to every congregation within a community, a uniqueness that goes beyond the personality of its primary leader and touches upon that congregation's unique set of passions and spiritual gifts. Therefore, each congregation should become fully engaged one with another, thus allowing the uniqueness of all to blend together as one for the benefit of their community. When viewed in this context, all the congregations (the Whole Church) of any given community become God's gift to the people of that community by which He desires to more fully reveal Himself.

A Pastor's Revelation about the Need for the Whole Church

Dave Runyon openly shares in the book *The Art of Neighboring* how his perception changed when he realized that the large church he was pastoring would never alone bring transformation to his community:

"Teaching in front of thousands of people felt like the opportunity of a lifetime. At least it did at first. And of course there were parts of my job that were exhilarating. On most nights, however, when I got into my car and drove home, I felt strangely empty. I knew what went in to putting on those services. We spent the majority of our time putting on an event that, to be honest, just didn't seem like it was producing the kind of life change we were hoping to see.

"My point is not to criticize large churches, because there are many good ones out there that are doing great things. Nor am I saying that large-group teaching isn't effective and that we should scrap it altogether. Instead I am saying that my experience as a large-church pastor caused me to reevaluate my thinking about transformation and the best ways to invest my time and energy. While I served there, a healthy sense of discontent grew in me. And over time I realized that our weekly service was always going to have limited impact in changing our community. I became convinced that no matter how much our church grew, a single congregation would never be able to truly transform our entire community.

"My healthy discontent sent me on a journey to redefine how I thought about the church and its ability to have a lasting impact. I left my teaching pastor position and found myself at another thriving church, where I continued to wrestle with the same gnawing thoughts and questions. I soon found myself becoming obsessed with John 17, an entire chapter that recounts Jesus' prayer just before He is arrested. First, Jesus prays for Himself, then for His disciples. Then He concludes by praying for us.

"What He prayed is powerful. He prayed that everyone who follows Him would be one; that we would be brought to complete unity. Jesus has a burning desire for there to be unity among *all* believers. In fact, He tells us that there is something so sacred and beautiful about oneness that it will draw people to God who aren't in a relationship with Him. This was the answer I was looking for to help facilitate lasting transformation in our city! And this is what prompted me to gather local pastors to listen to our mayor and to dream about what we could do together that we could never do alone." [12]

Section 2

Becoming the Incarnational Church

CHAPTER 11

NEIGHBORING IS A MOVE OF GOD
"Where Did This Movement Start?"

Dave Runyon's "healthy discontent," led him to ultimately see the divinely ordained significance of the Whole Church in his community working together. This perspective is growing in the hearts and minds of pastors and leaders all across our country today. This is the future for the church—the Whole Church working together in every neighborhood.

If you take time to stay current with the thoughts and discussions published in Christian literature and periodicals, or if you peruse the subject matter presented at church conferences and workshops, you will begin to catch a vision of what the Lord is doing in this season of Church history. He is challenging His Church to become more relational and incarnational, exhorting His people to demonstrate His love for humanity right where we live and work.

I did some cursory research about the Jesus Movement, a move of God that took place back in the late '60s and '70s. In so doing, I found it impossible to pinpoint exactly where it started. It was like little fires had broken out in various places around the country, and the accumulation of all these fires eventually became known as the Jesus Movement, a movement that swept thousands of souls into the Kingdom. And today, in much the same way, a neighboring movement is breaking out in different places across the country. Little fires are springing up. The Spirit is stirring once again!

How then does the Whole Church in a city move toward becoming the whole incarnational church of that city? Through my own experience, I have learned that there is no one way that leads to a collective incarnational work. I wish we had a road map for the journey, but it just isn't that straightforward. Moving away from the attractional church model and embracing the neighborhood model represents a profound change in the culture of a church. And it may take five to seven years to change that culture. Keep in mind, the current church model has been well entrenched for decades. It won't change overnight. Members of our congregations have grown comfortably accustomed to doing church in a somewhat passive style. But once leadership makes the commitment to move toward a neighboring style of ministry, members will find themselves being exhorted to start actively being representatives of the church right where they live and work. This will represent a clear departure from the past—a sea change, if you will—and it will likely take years to successfully change from the culture of the past. One thing is certain. Leadership will need to rely on the Lord every step of the way. It will become a season of faith and discovery.

Because we come from a "corporate" and "attractional" church mind-set, it may be challenging for some pastors to see the church in any other way than how they have always seen it. Rather than embrace the new, we all tend to default to our own familiar operating system. Change is never easy, even when we know the Lord may be in it. But I have talked with many pastors who are fully embracing this new movement, and they are ready for the new adventure. They welcome it on behalf of their congregation, and they look forward to working together with other pastors and churches in their city.

The remainder of this book is dedicated to those pastors and leaders who desire to join the Father in this new work that He is initiating—bringing His Whole Church together as one in order to reach our cities with the good news of God's Kingdom.

CHAPTER 12

GOD INITIATES A CITY MOVEMENT
"Lord, Are You Calling Me?"

When God is moved to do something here on earth, He is the one who takes the initiative. Throughout the Old Testament, whether it was Noah, Abraham, Moses, Gideon . . . you name the person, God always took the first step. It was no different in the days of the New Testament, and it is certainly no different today.

As the "favored" Noah was called to build an ark because of the wickedness of the human race (Genesis 6:1–8); as the "obedient" Abraham was uniquely called in Ur to become a father of a "great nation" (Hebrews 11:8); as the "very humble" Moses was called from the burning bush to lead God's people out of slavery in Egypt (Numbers 12:3; 11:1); as Gideon, the "mighty warrior," was called to deliver the Israelites from the Midianite's oppression (Judges 6:12); as the "highly favored" Mary was called to give birth to Jesus, the Son of God (Luke 1:28); as Peter was called to carry on Jesus' work (John 21:15–17); as Paul was called to the Gentiles (Acts 9:15), I believe that God calls someone to initiate and lead His work in a city. It is a high and lofty calling from God.

As I look at how God characterized some of those He called, I am taken aback by the thought that God would think so highly of them. In most cases, they were people of no great significance. Yet God saw something in their hearts that was attractive to Him.

This was the case with David, a lonely sheepherder, but he was a man after God's own heart, and he became the anointed king of Israel (Acts 13:22). This is the kind of leader God is looking for to lead a movement in every city, not one who pursues his own agenda, but one who seeks the Lord with all his heart and humbly serves Him.

When the Lord calls an individual, as He did with those mentioned above, the assignment is always impossible to accomplish—impossible, that is, without God. Humility is a priority when God makes His selection, because only a man with a humble heart recognizes that he is completely dependant on God for the task ahead. Humility, prayer, and a daily devotion to seek God's will . . . these are the traits of God's heroes. These are the hallmarks of those who changed the course of history in the past, and who will again change the course of history in the season ahead.

The individual that the Lord chooses to lead a citywide movement will be one whose path has already been marked out before him by the Lord for this good purpose. As the apostle points out, "For we are God's handiwork, created in Christ Jesus to do good works, which God prepared in advance for us to do" (Ephesians 2:10, NIV). As he responds to God's call, the citywide leader is only stepping into a destiny that the Lord planned for him long before he was even conceived.

God is looking for a leader who values the Whole Church in a city, just as Jesus did. If he is a pastor, he will see beyond his immediate congregation with a kingdom mind-set, demonstrating a caring concern for other pastors and advocating the advance of God's kingdom through the collective church. Because of his faithfulness and God's favor, he will eventually gain favor and support among other pastors and leaders.

I made a mistake once while working with a particular leader of a city. Unfortunately, I had not done my research. I assumed he was called and had credibility with other pastors, but he hadn't lived in the community long enough to build rapport or credibility. Needless to say, the citywide movement I had hoped for didn't materialize.

By the time it came to having someone lead the neighboring movement in our own community, I had come to learn that the person not only needed to be called by God, but needed to be someone that other pastors and leaders in the area respected. For years I watched Jeff Fisher, pastor of Hope Chapel in the San Fernando Valley, draw pastors together for a variety of events. I could plainly see that God's favor was with him, but more importantly, other pastors had come to realize what I had grown to see. When Jeff encouraged them to come together, many responded to his invitation, and even though he pastors a smaller congregation, it is clear to many in the surrounding area that God has given Jeff the call to lead a neighboring movement in our city.

I should add that a city leader does not need to be a pastor or even a pastor of a large congregation. In Fresno, California, God called Alan Doswald and Paul Haroutunian to lead the charge. Though neither Alan nor Paul is a pastor, it is clear to the pastoral leadership of that city that God has called them out to lead a neighboring movement in their city called "Loving our Neighbors."

He Gives the One He Calls Passion and Power

How does one know they are called to lead a movement like this in their city? I am sure there are many indicators for a future leader of a city neighborhood movement, but experience has taught me that there are two primary indicators. First, God makes His calling very clear to the leader himself. And secondly, other leaders will begin to confirm that call.

It might be helpful to remind ourselves what the apostle Paul had to say to our brethren at Philippi on the subject of God working within those He calls. Through my years of ministry, I have found this directive to be of great personnel comfort in my attempts to determine the Lord's plan for my own life:

> "Work out your salvation with fear and trembling; for it is God who is at *work in you*, both to *will* and *work* for His *good pleasure*" (Philippians 2:12–13 NASB).

The second use of the word *work* in these verses refers to God's operation in your soul. The word *will* has to do with desire or passion. In other words, this work is something that you desire to do, because of your special calling from God and the work He is doing in your heart. And the third appearance of the word *work* is the Greek word *energeo*, from which we get our word *energy*. Because of the divine calling, God gives you the energy or power to carry out this good work, and it is all for His "good pleasure." In other words, God's operation as a city leader is initiated by God working in you, giving you a desire or passion for the work, and then, being yoked with Jesus, He gives you the energy to carry it out to serve His good pleasure or purpose.

Without a deep "desire" from God and His "energy," the ministry of a city leader will be tiresome and pointless. When the hand of God is absent from the work, the city leader will find himself under a heavy yoke. But when our Lord is engaged in the process, the work becomes effortless.

God Initiates a City Movement

When God calls us from one ministry to a new focus of ministry, He will change the desires of our heart. He will also begin to withhold His energy or ability to do work that once seemed effortless. When we labor in ministry in our own strength we will find it difficult to do even the smallest things.

After twenty-seven years as the associate pastor of the Valley Vineyard Church in Reseda, God pulled the plug on my desire to do the work that I had carried out by His grace for so many years. I had a new passion that the Lord had given me that was supplanting my desire for local church ministry. I couldn't deny that the passion was gone after all those years. I didn't feel like I belonged in the role anymore. My calling had given way to a new passion for what is now called Neighborhood Initiative. Before I took the step of faith, I remember struggling with this thought: "Where will the resources come from if I leave the security of my paid position?" As I continued to struggle, I began to wonder if I was wrestling with the fear of not receiving a paycheck on a regular basis. As someone who had counseled so many within the church to have faith that God would provide, the matter became an integrity issue for me as I began to examine my own lack of trust. It was about this time that the Lord made it even more difficult for me. He very clearly communicated to me, "If you want to stay with the old thing then you are on your own." The Lord had me over a barrel, but I continued to hang on to the old because of my financial insecurities. Then one Sunday morning, our pastor, Bill Dwyer, gave a message entitled, "Going All In on Life." As he spoke, I knew the Lord was speaking directly to me about going "all in" with Neighborhood Initiative. When Bill shared how Elisha slaughtered his oxen and used his plow to cook the meat, I knew that the Lord was calling me to a new identity. But

He wasn't just calling me to a new identity. He was challenging me to trust Him to provide just as Elisha did when he burned his only means (plow and oxen) to provide for his family.

The Lord could not have been any clearer that day. He was calling me to step away from the security of my paid position and to entrust my future to Him. I went home that day and shared this revelation with my wife who simply said, "I will follow you wherever you go." This was indeed confirmation that I was on the right path. Then, to my complete and utter surprise, the leadership of our church decided to continue my salary for seven months! And they even told me that I could continue to use my old office! What marvelous provision and blessing through a simple step of faith. And I never would have experienced it had I not trusted God.

He Births a City Movement through the One He Calls

A move of God starts small. God plants His seed of an idea in the heart of someone, and that seed begins to grow. Often He plants a similar seed in the hearts of others who then join in the work. God can communicate His plan in a variety of ways. But in each case, thoughts begin to develop and eventually ideas give way to discussions with God, trusted family members, and friends about this vision that just won't go away. In many cases it is quite exciting, but on the other hand, like with Moses, it can be threatening. When shared, the vision may not always be well received, even by those who are closest to us. We see an example of this with Joseph and his brothers, and we see it again in the life of Jesus. The Father had sent Him on a mission to reconcile the world to Himself and "even his own brothers did not believe in him" (John 7:5, NIV). Likewise, those called to shepherd a citywide movement may not receive a welcoming response, but we must keep in mind that we have been called upon to give birth to a movement ordained by God, and it is our responsibility to steward it toward maturity. Over time, the movement will begin to take form and grow. Eventually, more and more people see the merits of what God is bringing forth, and before long you have a full-blown movement. Those who have experienced the birthing of one of God's visions can relate to this process. There are times in the early stages when we may question the vision, but then the Lord will use someone or something to confirm His work. We never need to defend what He is doing. We need only to trust Him to grow and mature that which He has begun.

Keep in mind, the enemy will do everything in his power to kill the vision that is being birthed, much as he did with Jesus when He was just an infant. The enemy is dead set against God's purposes, and he will do everything possible to derail a citywide movement. He may use a close friend, just like he used Peter to question Jesus. He is shrewd and cunning, and he knows how to discourage. This is why intercessory prayer is so vital to birthing and maintaining a citywide neighborhood ministry. From beginning to maturity, the entire process must be bathed in prayer.

CHAPTER 13

DO WHAT THE FATHER'S DOING
"How Do I Do This?"

Just how does a citywide leader navigate the challenges of encouraging neighborhood ministry throughout a city? The best model for this new journey is the ministry of our Lord as He visited one city after another during His three years of earthly ministry.

Dallas Willard always emphasized, "Don't ever try to make anything happen." Dallas was certainly not a self-promoter, yet his influence with pastors and church leaders around the world has been profound. Trying to make something happen only produces Ishmaels. Sarah was unwilling to wait on God for the child of promise, so she coerced Abraham into marrying Hagar. This fleshly effort on Sarah's part has caused all kinds of problems that persist to this very day.

Sarah-like attempts to make something happen in our cities will only produce frustration, fruitless results, and conflict in relationships. But joining the Father in what He is already doing produces peace of mind, harmony, and brings Him greater glory. This is exactly what Jesus modeled during His ministry here on earth:

> "My Father is always at his work to this very day, and I, too, am working . . . Very truly I tell you, the Son can do nothing by himself; he can do only what he sees his

Father doing, because whatever the Father does the Son also does. For the Father loves the Son and shows him all he does. Yes, and he will show him even greater works than these, so that you will be amazed" (John 5:17, 19–20 NIV).

If Jesus could do nothing by Himself, then certainly we as pastors and leaders must become equally dependent, joining with the Father where He is already at work, if we truly want to see our cities transformed.

Our Lord lived out His earthly ministry as His Father presented Him with one divine opportunity after another. Jesus wasn't out to make things happen, but joined with His Father in what He was doing. I have come to refer to this as a *"Kairos Life."* Most of us are driven by the clock, by busy schedules consisting of deadlines and personal agendas. But Jesus lived His life free of these constraints. The activities of Jesus' life were driven by His relationship with His Father, His sensitivity to the Spirit, and His loving service to the people around Him. He had no schedule or itinerary. Thus He was free to respond in accordance with each and every situation that confronted Him. This is the *kairos* life.

What Is *Kairos*?

The Greek has two words for time: *chronos* and *kairos*. *Chronos* concerns the linear passage of time, like the time we experience in the twenty-four-hour day. We define our workweeks by the number of hours that we work. We have a list of things to do and only so much time to get everything done. This is *chronos* time. Having a *chronos* mind-set focuses us on time as the controlling factor for our activities, thereby causing us to miss out on many spur-of-the-moment opportunities. Instead of seeing what our Father is doing all around us, our eyes are trained on the clock, where we need to go next, or checking off another item on our "to do list."

Kairos is quite different than *chronos*. It is not linear. It doesn't include a clock or a schedule. It is living life in the moment, being fully present when you are with people just as Jesus was. It involves living an unhurried life. *Kairos* is best referred to as an "opportunity." For example, when Jesus sat down at the well of Sychar, He beheld an opportunity to converse with the Samaritan woman. This was a *kairos* moment which His disciples missed. They were on *chronos* time, busying themselves with purchasing food, unaware of the tremendous opportunity that the encounter with this woman would afford.

The apostle Paul wrote, "Wake up, sleeper, rise from the dead, and Christ will shine on you. Be very careful, then, how you live—not as unwise but as wise, making the most of every opportunity [*kairos*] . . . " (Ephesians 5:14–16, NIV). Here Paul is exhorting followers of Christ (and I believe his exhortation applies even more so to Christian leaders) not to sleep through opportunities and thereby miss out on what God is doing in that particular moment. Busyness and laziness are two of the biggest culprits to diverting our eyes from seeing what God is doing. We find a similar exhortation in Colossians 4:5 (NIV): "Be wise in the way you act towards outsiders; make the most of every opportunity [*kairos*]." Paul is giving us a window into the kind of life he lived during his years of ministry, no doubt the same kind that Jesus lived.

The funny thing about *kairos* moments is that they are often viewed as intrusions in our lives. They frequently occur when we least expect them, and they seldom fit into our self-determined plan for the day. Each time one occurs, we are forced to make a choice. Do I continue, or do I disrupt my plans and choose to lay them aside for the sake of what God is doing in the moment?

I have often thought that when Jesus gave the parable of the Good Samaritan, He was making a comparison between the way He lived His life and the way the religious leaders of His day lived theirs (Luke 10:25-37). The priest and the Levite were too busy after their temple service activities to stop and care for their desperate "neighbor" who was beaten, robbed, and left to die by the side of the road. Oddly enough, Jesus used a member of the most despised society for the Jew of that day, the Samaritan, to demonstrate extraordinary "neighbor-love." The religious leaders missed out on the *kairos* moment. Their *chronos* mindset spurred them down the road. Maybe they viewed it as an inconvenience, an obstruction to their getting home on time, or an unplanned interruption to their schedule for that day. Maybe they thought there was too much risk involved. Some speculate there was a religious law that one who was engaged in religious ceremonials was not to touch a human body twenty-four hours before the ceremony. Whatever the reason, they could not be bothered, and as a result, they missed a perfectly good opportunity to lovingly minister to someone in need.

You may be asking now, "So, how does one enter into the *kairos* life, especially as a pastor or leader of a community?"

During the early development of Neighborhood Initiative the Lord helped me understand that there were two ways I could choose to move forward with this good work that He had initiated. I could try and make things happen on my own, like Sarah did with Abraham, or I could join Him in what He was doing. This choice is at the very heart of the *kairos* lifestyle. I discovered the first approach was difficult and frustrating and the second was easy and full of wonderful surprises. It is life in the "easy yoke" of our Lord.

Not trying to make something happen is such a freeing way to live life. I have found there are three things I can do that have enabled me to live a life free of a performance attitude and a mind-set of "trying to make something happen." These three simple steps have allowed me to see what the Father is doing right in my own neighborhood.

I pray

On most Tuesday mornings I walk through my neighborhood, and I pray for each of my neighbors by name, asking the Lord to show me what He is doing in their lives. Sometimes He will speak to me about one of my neighbors or give me ideas of what He would like me to do or to say. In all honesty, there are also days when I don't hear anything. Nothing seems to be happening. On one such occasion, I prayed out to God, "Is this just a fruitless activity?" That very night, God answered my prayer. I found myself actively engaged in conversation with my neighbor from directly across the street. Though my efforts may have seemed fruitless that morning, the spiritual repercussions of that evening conversation continue to this very day. Week after week, He continues to faithfully and dramatically demonstrate that He is walking with me as I pray for my neighbors.

I wait

After I pray, I wait for God to respond. In the flesh, it is natural for us to attempt to stir up activities that will create connections. But I have learned (the hard way!) the value of waiting upon

Him. This kind of waiting is not a passive waiting, but a waiting with a sense of expectation. It is the type of waiting that Isaiah speaks of when he says,

> Yet those who wait for the LORD
> Will gain new strength;
> They will mount up *with* wings like eagles,
> They will run and not get tired,
> They will walk and not become weary. (Isaiah 40:31, NASB)

Isaiah is referring to the faithful and watchful waiting of those who fully expect God to respond. They do not grow weary in their waiting. In fact, they grow in spiritual strength. This is the kind of waiting I do. I pray, and then I wait for the Father to respond.

I watch

I have prayed. I have waited. Now I observe, watching for obvious signs that the Father is at work. Out of nowhere, usually when least expected, something will happen. A neighbor will call me and ask me to perform a wedding at his home, or another might ask me to officiate at a funeral. A tree might get blown down on a neighbor's house, crushing a car in the process. Someone has a health scare and an ambulance gets called to the scene. All of these become God-ordained opportunities to enter into relationship with our neighbors. We can't make these situations happen on our own. But He, in response to our prayers, permits these *kairos* moments to occur in order that we might enter into a life where He is already at work.

Whether it is in your own neighborhood or as a leader of a

citywide movement, these three simple steps will start you on your path to intersect with what God wants to do in your city. Again, you don't have to make anything happen in your own strength. Just pray, wait with anticipation, watch to see what He is doing, and then join in.

Living this kind of life with the Father is like a little kid waiting for his dad to invite him on some new excursion. He knows that only Dad can drive the car, and he waits for his dad to say, "Come on, kid! I have a wonderful surprise for you. Let's go!" And off they go together with Dad in the driver's seat. This is the adventure I spoke of earlier. This is the *kairos* life: becoming like a child and enjoying the ride with Dad on an amazing journey in ministry in your city.

I firmly believe that it is this simple childlike attitude that lies at the heart of Kingdom living. Jesus said, "Truly I tell you, unless you change and become like little children, you will never enter the kingdom of heaven. Therefore, whoever takes the lowly position of this child is the greatest in the kingdom of heaven." (Matthew 18:3–4 NIV). Jesus is saying that the way we gain access into the Kingdom is the very same way we live in the Kingdom. When we live like a child, we find it easy to join Him in His earthly work. But when we get away from childlikeness, we start doing our own thing, thereby distancing ourselves from what the Father is doing. Once you understand what Dallas was saying about not making something happen, then you as a pastor or leader in your city are in a place to join the Father in what He wants to do through you in your city.

CHAPTER 14

WAR ROOM
Where Do I Start?

> Then he [Jesus] said to his disciples, "The harvest is plentiful but the workers are few. Ask the Lord of the harvest, therefore, to send out workers into his harvest field."
> —Matthew 9:37–38 NIV

I was deeply moved by the character of Miss Clara in the movie *War Room*, an elderly but passionate intercessor. Through her role, we see the effect that someone can have on the world around them when they retreat into their prayer closet (Miss Clara's "war room") and fervently pray. It would do the church well today if all of us were exhorted to pray with the same kind of fervency and expectation.

In a military context, a war room is where strategy is planned and current battle situations are monitored. In the movie, Miss Clara applied the same principles to her spiritual life. She constantly monitored the spiritual battlefield around her, praying accordingly, and then watched to see what God would do in response to her prayers.

Unfortunately, few in the church today recognize that we are in a battle. But as Paul reminded us, "Our struggle is not against flesh and blood, but against the rulers, against the authorities, against the powers of this dark world and against the spiritual forces of evil in the heavenly realms. . . . and pray in the Spirit on all occasions with all kinds of prayers and requests. With this in mind, be alert and always keep on praying for all the Lord's people" (Ephesians 6:12, 18). From Paul's perspective, it is through prayer that we engage the spiritual forces of darkness, thus enabling us to monitor what is going on in the battle for our cities and better prepare us to participate in God's strategy.

Spiritual warfare associated with what God is doing in bringing His Church together incarnationally in neighborhoods has been very real. There have been deaths, divorce, cancer, tension in relationships, and so much more. I hesitate to say too much more, because I know the enemy would love for us to obsess on his activity. I agree with what C. S. Lewis espouses: "There are two equal and opposite errors into which our race can fall about the devils. One is to disbelieve in their existence. The other is to believe, and to feel an excessive and unhealthy interest in them. They themselves are equally pleased by both errors, and hail a materialist or magician with the same delight."[13]

Without prayer, which is a key weapon in our war chest, we are like a soldier going to battle without a weapon. Prayer is a mighty instrument that God has given us to tap into His power (Ephesians 3:14–21). Mary, Queen of Scots was well aware of the power that was released when a faithful man of God prayed: "I fear the prayers of John Knox more than all the assembled armies of Europe."[14] John Knox is considered to be the greatest Reformer in the history of Scotland. "Perhaps more than anything else, John Knox is known for his prayer 'Give me Scotland, or I die.' Knox's prayer was not an arrogant demand, but the passionate plea of a man willing to die for the sake of the pure preaching of the Gospel and the salvation of his countrymen. Knox's greatness lay in his humble dependence on our sovereign God to save His people, revive a nation, and reform His Church."[15]

Knox, like many other notable church reformers and movement leaders, had a passion for God and His ability to bring reformation and change to a nation. A. T. Pierson, leader of the modern missions movement, declared, "From the Day of Pentecost, there has not been one great spiritual awakening in any land which has not begun in a union of prayer, though only among two or three; no such outward, upward movement has continued after such prayer meetings have declined."[16]

In the human soul there is resistance to this powerful weapon. Let's be honest. We pastors and leaders and those in God's Church would prefer to do almost anything than attend a prayer gathering. Our flesh loathes the thought of prayer. We have all attended prayer gatherings that have dwindled in size. Enthusiasm is stirred initially, but after a time there are only the faithful few left standing. Why?

General William Booth, founder of the Salvation Army movement, gave answer to this question: "You must pray with all your might. That does not mean saying your prayers, or sitting gazing about in church or chapel with eyes wide open while someone else says them for you. It means fervent, effectual, untiring wrestling with God . . . This kind of prayer be sure the devil and the world and your own indolent, unbelieving nature will oppose. They will pour water on this flame."[17] These three—the devil, the world, and the flesh—war against us believers getting into our "war room" or gathering with other saints to participate in the most powerful activity in this world. And yet when we evaluate it on the surface, it seems so inconsequential. However, our Lord says, "But when you pray, go into your room, close the door and pray to your Father, who is unseen. Then your Father, who sees what is done in secret, will reward you" (Matthew 6:6 NIV). That reward comes now, in this life. A life of prayerlessness yields nothing.

Jesus' half-brother James ("camel's knees" as he was referred to in his day because of his life of prayer on his knees) states, "The *effective, fervent* prayer of a righteous man avails much" (James 5:16 NKJV). What kind of praying? Fervent praying. The word *fervent* that James uses here literally means "boiling, hot, glowing." Figuratively it means "violent, impetuous, furious, or impassioned." James is talking about passionate praying.

In the movie *War Room*, Miss Clara embodies this passion when she prays, a kind of prayer that is missing in most churches today. James also uses the word "effectual." He is saying the passionate praying of a righteous person is successful in producing a desired or intended result. Miss Clara's passionate prayers produced the desired results.

In the context of neighborhood ministry, we must take into consideration the probable results of fervent, impassioned prayers on behalf of those living around us. What might happen if churches began targeting specific neighborhoods with prayer? What might happen in the homes of our neighbors if we began interceding for them on a regular basis?

CHAPTER 15

SUSTAINED SEASON OF PRAYER
"Who Prays Like That?"

In the early days, when I was a college pastor, we as a congregation went through a very lengthy sustained season of prayer, and we saw incredible things happen in and through our congregation. We would come together on Wednesday evenings for teaching. Afterward, we would gather for an extended time of prayer. There was a great sense of God's presence and a strong desire to come together to pray. It wasn't something that was generated by man, but a unique move of God. It was during the early days of the Jesus Movement and God was moving in a powerful way.

At the heart of this sustained season of prayer was an eighty-year-old woman, Grandma Kelly as we fondly called her. I remember her saying, "I feel like a young woman trapped in this old body." Though old physically, she was spiritually vibrant. She would wake early each morning and pray for hours for our pastor and staff and our church. She was one amazing woman of God, and I am sure she received a "rich welcome" when she entered into heaven. Looking back on Grandma Kelly's ministry, I firmly believe that her passionate prayers opened the doors for our season of sustaining prayer.

Jeremiah Lanphier, like Grandma Kelly, understood the power that is released when God's people come together to pray. J. Edwin Orr tells his story:

"This is a record of something God did 130 years ago in New York City. It illustrates how God has started every harvest time in history, through the concerted prayer of his people. Toward the middle of the last century (19th), the glow of earlier religious awakenings had faded. America was prosperous and felt little need to call on God. But in the 1850s, secular and religious conditions combined to bring about a crash. The third great panic in American history swept the giddy structure of speculative wealth away. Thousands of merchants were forced to the wall as banks failed and railroads went into bankruptcy. Factories were shut down and vast numbers thrown out of employment, New York City alone having 30,000 idle men. In October 1857, the hearts of people were thoroughly weaned from speculation and uncertain gain, while hunger and despair stared them in the face.

On 1st July, 1857, a quiet and zealous businessman named Jeremiah Lanphier took up an appointment as a City Missionary in downtown New York. Lanphier was appointed by the North Church of the Dutch Reformed denomination. This church was suffering from depletion of membership due to the removal of the population from the downtown to the better residential quarters, and the new City Missionary was engaged to make diligent visitation in the immediate neighborhood with a view to enlisting church attendance among the floating population of the lower city. The Dutch Consistory felt that it had appointed an ideal layman for the task in hand, and so it was.

"Burdened so by the need, Jeremiah Lanphier decided to invite others to join him in a noonday prayer meeting, to be held on Wednesdays once a week. He therefore distributed a handbill:

HOW OFTEN SHALL I PRAY?

As often as the language of prayer is in my heart; as often as I see my need of help; as often as I feel the power of temptation; as often as I am made sensible of any spiritual declension or feel the aggression of a worldly spirit.

In prayer we leave the business of time for that of eternity, and intercourse with men for intercourse with God.

A day prayer meeting is held every Wednesday, from 12 to 1 o'clock, in the Consistory building in the rear of the North Dutch Church, corner of Fulton and William Streets (entrance from Fulton and Ann Streets).

This meeting is intended to give merchants, mechanics, clerks, strangers, and businessmen generally an opportunity to stop and call upon God amid the perplexities incident to their respective avocations. It will continue for one hour; but it is also designed for those who may find it inconvenient to remain more than five or ten minutes, as well as for those who can spare the whole hour.

"Accordingly at twelve noon, 23rd September, 1857 the door was opened, and the faithful Lanphier took his seat to await the response to his invitation. Five minutes went by. No one appeared. The missionary paced the room in a conflict of fear and faith. Ten minutes elapsed. Still no one came. Fifteen minutes passed. Lanphier was yet alone. Twenty minutes; twenty-five; thirty; and then at 12.30 p.m., a step was heard on the stairs, and the first person appeared, then another, and another, and another, until six people were present and the prayer meeting began. On the following Wednesday, October 7th, there were forty intercessors.

"Thus in the first week of October 1857, it was decided to hold a meeting daily instead of weekly. Within six months, *ten thousand businessmen* were gathering daily for prayer in New York, and within two years, a million converts were added to the American churches.

"Undoubtedly the greatest revival in New York's colorful history was sweeping the city, and it was of such an order to make the whole nation curious. There was no fanaticism, no hysteria, simply an incredible movement of the people to pray."[18]

A movement like this is undoubtedly needed in our nation today. It starts with those who are convinced that God works powerfully through the prayers of His saints.

When people from my present congregation started all-night prayer meetings for our city back in May of 2000, Dallas Willard said, "Give it five years." At the time it didn't sit well with us. The all-night prayer meetings continued for a season and eventually transitioned into pastors and leaders praying together weekly. Our objective was to come together to pray for churches throughout our Valley, and for our city; to develop caring relationships with one another; and to wait on the Lord to show us what He wanted us to do together in our city. After more than a decade of prayer, Neighborhood Initiative surfaced as God's desired plan.

We have continued to pray together over all these years. There are ebbs and flows to the number that join us each week, but the point is this: we have remained faithful to Him in prayer and are waiting and watching to see what He will do in response to our years of praying together.

If we want to see God move in our cities, we need to not only spend more time in our own prayer closets, but we also need to come together with other believers and pray like those reformers did in the past. With the anti-Christian sentiment growing in our nation today, we pastors and leaders need to gather and pray like those in the early church:

> "'Now, Lord, consider their threats and enable your servants to speak your word with great boldness. Stretch out your hand to heal and perform signs and wonders through the name of your holy servant Jesus.' After they prayed, the place where they were meeting was shaken. And they were all filled with the Holy Spirit and spoke the word of God boldly" (Acts 4:29–31, NIV).

This is our starting point for a neighboring movement in our cities. It was in this context of intercessory prayer that the Church was birthed and continued to advance throughout the known world.

CHAPTER 16

GOD MOVES AT THE SPEED OF RELATIONSHIP

"How Does a City Movement Grow?"

> "Though it is the smallest of all seeds, yet when it grows, it is the largest of garden plants and becomes a tree, so that the birds come and perch in its branches." He told them still another parable: "The kingdom of heaven is like yeast that a woman took and mixed into about sixty pounds of flour until it worked all through the dough."
> —Matthew 13:32–33 NIV

A city neighboring movement starts small and grows little by little, but it has the potential to take over an entire community. Because it starts small, the neighboring movement is counterintuitive to what we typically look for in a church program or activity. Generally speaking, the church is always looking for the next big event to spark something even bigger, yet Jesus tells us that it starts like a tiny mustard seed. It starts small in each of us and by God's power has the potential to change the culture of churches, relationships between churches, and the communities where we live. As God's kingdom work grows in us, and then through us, it will accomplish the construction of Christ's intended church, one of flesh that extends to hearts outside our facilities and well-designed programs, meeting people where they are just as Christ did.

Jesus likened the kingdom of God to yeast. Yeast is a living organism that forms colonies of single, simple cells. Like the tiny mustard seed that grows into a large tree, when just a small amount of yeast is kneaded into flour and water it will eventually permeate the entire lump. And in the same way that yeast effects flour, God's kingdom has the potential to transform an entire city when added in just one neighborhood at a time.

Some years back, I was teaching a seminar on neighboring in Denver. At the end of the seminar, the facilitator opened up a time for questions and answers. A woman raised her hand and asked me, "How can loving my neighbors have any impact on the city of Denver?" I responded to her question by referring to the parable of the mustard seed and the yeast; that if she loved her neighbors, eventually the seed or yeast of her love would impact all of Denver. Now, that may sound like an overstatement, but Jesus knew that love of this nature is contagious, even if it began with a single person. In time, others will begin to jump onboard, and before long you have a movement that has spread throughout a community.

My good friend Fred West once told me that "God moves at the speed of relationship." He is so right. It is only as relationships among pastors and leaders grow and the vision of neighboring begins to multiply, that people in their churches will begin to love their neighbors, and the Kingdom of God advances little by little. But it is important for us to remember that relationships take time to develop and that change of this nature develops slowly.

As Tom Anthony once said, "You can change church structure overnight, but it takes five to seven years to change church culture." Moving away from the attractional model to become a relational or incarnational church will take time, because God only moves as fast as you and your congregation develop those new relationships. Eventually, with lots of prayerful pastoring, those relationships will "infect" the entire congregation. And once they catch hold of the neighboring movement, they won't want to go back to the old way of doing things.

CHAPTER 17

THERE IS NO ONE WAY TO DO THIS
"What Are Ways That This Neighboring Movement Grows?"

When I first started with Neighborhood Initiative, I assumed there was only *one* way to introduce neighboring to the Church. But my eyes have been opened to see that our Lord is very creative. He loves diversity. When God gets involved, He does the unimaginable. I am constantly fascinated with the creative ways He has worked through people to move neighboring along. We like our programs where one size fits all, but God wants to work uniquely through each of us to bring about what He desires in a neighborhood, a church, and with the Whole Church in a city. I have watched the neighborhood movement unfold through the years, and I am in awe as to how the Spirit of God has worked through different people in His Church to bring about something unique and beautiful. We are left with exclaiming, "God did that!"

In a Congregation

I was once asked by a pastor how I would suggest introducing neighborhood ministry into his congregation. As I began to respond to his question, he pulled out a note pad and began taking notes. After I finished, I asked if he could type it up and e-mail it to me. Here is what he sent to me:

A Suggested Plan to Implement NI in a Local Congregation

1. Seed the Neighborhood Initiative book into key leaders such as staff, elders, church leaders, etc. Optional: use *Living a Kairos Life*, a leader's and participant's guide for the NI book.
2. Select a point person/community pastor from among the key leaders, or any other person who emerges with leadership potential and a passion for NI.
3. Geographic small groups: If your small groups are already set up geographically, begin to introduce your NI plan with your existing small groups.
4. If your small groups are not presently set up geographically, map out and identify the most densely populated areas where people from your church live to locate where to plant "community groups."
5. Appoint community group leaders.
6. Start the community/neighborhood group.
   a. Start to pray for that region.
   b. Take the community group through *Neighborhood Initiative and the Love of God* using the *Living a Kairos Life* leader's and participant's guides.
   c. Encourage relationship building among the community group members and with their neighbors. (Refer to NI Resources for ideas.)
   d. Seek out other believers in your neighborhood and begin to develop relationship with them. You might want to start a neighborhood house of prayer.

e. Begin to identify six types of people among the community group members:
      i. Prayers—People who have a passion for prayer and will encourage others to pray.
      ii. Relaters—People who love people: relational networkers.
      iii. Belongers—People who love to put on events; hospitality and helping people belong is their passion.
      iv. Servers—People who love to meet the needs of other people in the community and will encourage others to do the same.
      v. Disciple-makers—People who love to share the Gospel.
      vi. Growers—People who love to see people grow in the Lord: Disciplers.
      vii. Host regular events to foster belonging among neighbors from the community such as barbeques, block parties, etc. This will help people feel included.
7. Start Bible discussion based groups to get people exploring and experiencing Jesus.

While all that I laid out that day might represent a good means to introduce a congregation to neighborhood ministry, there is an inherent problem. The thoughts and ideas were mine. In order for neighborhood ministry to effectively take root in a congregation, the Spirit needs to birth it through a pastor or leader of that congregation. You might benefit from some of those ideas I have shared above, but in the final analysis, you will need to seek the Lord's plans for your own flock.

In a Neighborhood

I was asked by Phil Miglioratti of the Mission America Coalition to facilitate a neighboring sphere for Love2020. In 2012, MAC launched Love2020 a national campaign to draw together ministries, churches, whole denominations, and individual Christians to show the love of Christ to every person in America by the end of the decade. Love2020 has thirty-some affinity spheres, and neighboring is one of them. I was quite honored to be asked. Prayer, Care, Share is at the heart of MAC to reach those outside of faith in Jesus Christ. Each of the sphere facilitators was asked to write up a plan for Prayer, Care, Share that could be put on a separate page of the Love2020 website. The following is the plan I submitted:

NEIGHBORHOOD SPHERE
PRAYER, CARE, SHARE STATEMENT

PRAYER
"Devote yourselves to prayer, being watchful and thankful"
(Colossians 4:2, NIV).

Prayer for our cities begins at home and in our neighborhoods. Here's a simple plan for "Prayer Walking Your Neighborhood":

- **Pray** for your neighbors by name, considering their physical and spiritual needs, concerns, and health. Ask the Lord to show you what He is doing in your neighborhood. While you are walking and praying, engage any neighbors you may meet along the way.

- **Wait** on God. Your Father is already at work in your neighborhood. Wait for Him to invite you into what He is doing. This is a waiting with great anticipation.

- **Watch** to see what the Father is doing. As you are praying, He may reveal things through something He puts on your heart or speak to you as you talk to a neighbor or as you see a need.

- **Join** your Father as He invites you into what He is doing in your neighborhood. Enjoy the adventure!

CARE

"When he saw the crowds, he had compassion on them, because they were harassed and helpless, like sheep without a shepherd" (Matthew 9:36, NIV).

Care flows from a heart that is filled with compassion for those in your home and neighborhood. If you love them as yourself, your heart will go out to those in your neighborhood. As you pray for them, you will begin to care for them the way you care for yourself.

Here's where you start:

- **Co-laboring with God.** Once the Lord invites you into what He is doing, recognize that this is His doing and that He will give you the grace to care for those in your neighborhood.

- **Initiate conversation.** The needs of neighbors are manifold. All you need to do is take some time to talk with your neighbors, and before long they will fill you in on the needs of others who live on your block. Invite neighbors over for dinner or coffee and they will open up like a flower about what is going on in their hearts, their families, and the things that concern them most.

- **Listen.** Learn to ask good questions and then listen. Did I say listen? Resist trying to interject things to say while they are talking. It shuts down the flow of things coming from their heart. Offer to pray for them if it seems appropriate.

- **Meet the Need.** When a neighbor's need becomes apparent, meet the need. They will never listen to our words until they know we really care. Meeting the need may be just listening, or helping with something around their home, or providing food for them. Caring for them opens their hearts to relationship. Don't be surprised if they want to help you. On the other hand, don't be surprised if they never offer to help you.

- **You can't do everything.** Keep in mind that every need in your neighborhood is not your responsibility. Sometimes you will have to say no. A neighbor may want to take advantage of your kind heart, and that's where you need to be as wise as a serpent and innocent as a dove. For some, this may be hard, but you want to be about your Father's business.

- **You may need a partner.** Enlist others in your neighborhood to help you with larger tasks. Look for helpful neighbors who would like to help you bear the burden of a needy neighbor. Don't do it alone.

You will burn out and give up on caring for your neighbors.

SHARE

"And pray for us, too, that God may open a door for our message, so that we may proclaim the mystery of Christ."
(Colossians 4:3, NIV).

If you look at the accounts of Jesus sharing about Himself and the Gospel of the kingdom, you will never see Him do it the same way twice. No, never. Sometimes an account happened with very few words, like the man next to Him on the cross, but on other occasions they were lengthier. I love observing how He beautifully revealed who He was to the woman at the well. He was a master of the moment for sharing the Gospel. The Lord will give you these kinds of moments with your neighbors. It may be in a one-on-one situation, over a meal, in a small group setting . . . you name it.

Be ready to give an Answer.

When God opens a door for the Gospel, allow the Holy Spirit to speak through you as you share your story and then His story. We see the apostle Paul using this approach in the book of Acts. Become effective in sharing the Gospel in this manner with your neighbors. Role-playing is a very helpful tool for training.

Here are a few pointers for getting started:

- **Share your story.**

    Write out your story and include these three parts:

- What your life was like before you met Jesus.
- How you came into a relationship with Him.
- What your life is like now that you have Him in your life.
- Be able to share your story in just a few minutes, depending on the situation.

• **Share His story.**

- Read the Gospels so you become familiar with the big picture of Jesus' life, ministry, the cross, and resurrection.
- Memorize verses that you can share when you are imparting the Gospel. The more verses you memorize the freer you are when sharing the Gospel.
- Of course, you can take them to one of the Gospels and let them read it (or you can read it) and give their impressions as they read. So often, we want to give our understanding first, but allow them to respond with their thoughts. When they begin to ask you questions, then you have earned the right to speak. (See 1 Peter 3:15.)

• **Listen to their response.**

Ask them their response to what they have heard or read to see if they are receptive and open to the Lord.

• **If they are responsive, stay with them.**

If they listen to you and what they have heard, stay with that person, as Jesus said. You have found a person of peace. Devote time to the relationship and help them in their new walk with the Lord.

I offer the above only as a helpful tool for those involved in neighborhood ministry; however, each of us will need to move out into our own neighborhoods in accordance with the way the Spirit of God leads us individually. *Neighborhood Initiative and the Love of God* and the NI website (neighborhoodinitiative.org) provide a wealth of suggestions and helps for connecting with your neighbors, but these are only helps. The best suggestions will come from the Helper, the Holy Spirit, as you submit to His lead and ask for insight as to how best to reach your neighbor with the love of the Father.

Remember, the neighboring movement is not a program, but an organic work of God. For those of us who have grown dependent on church programs, it might prove a little difficult for us to assume that there is no one way to do this neighboring thing. Other churches in your community might develop methods of reaching neighbors that vary drastically from your own. But that's okay. The goal is not to reproduce identical methods in every neighborhood. The goal is to reflect the love of God in one neighborhood after another and to lead people out of darkness into the light of our Father's Kingdom.

In the following section you will have an opportunity to observe the diversity and creative handiwork of God through His people.

SECTION 3

Stories of the Lord's Incarnational Work in Cities

CHAPTER 18

THE LORD'S WORK IN THE LORD'S WAY

"How Is the Lord Doing This?"

"I will build my church, and the gates of Hades will not overcome it."
—Matthew 16:18, NIV

Years ago, I was introduced to a message given by Dr. Francis Schaeffer entitled, "The Lord's Work in the Lord's Way." I was deeply impacted by what he presented and have listened to it over and over again. At the heart of his message, Schaeffer stressed the importance of quietly and humbly waiting in prayer for the Holy Spirit to do His work through His people. In his opinion, the greatest threat to Christianity is when those in Christian ministry attempt to do the Lord's work in their own strength. He compares doing the Lord's work in the flesh with Napoleon, who, in Schaeffer's opinion, was the personification of human pride. With his hand tucked into his coat, Schaeffer perceives Napoleon as saying, "I do this! I have done this! I will do this!" In contrast, Schaeffer points to our Lord in the Garden of Gethsemane saying, "Not my will, but your will be done." This is the attitude we need to see in the neighboring movement: His will being done. His work done in His way.

What follows is a series of stories, each very different from the other, but all giving testimony to the Lord's work and the Church becoming incarnational in the neighborhood.

CHAPTER 19

PIONEERING A CITYWIDE NEIGHBORING MOVEMENT AND BEYOND

Dave Runyon, Art of Neighboring and CityUnite, Denver, Colorado

Dave Runyon is one of the pioneers in the neighborhood movement, so it seems only fitting that we begin this section with the story of how God has greatly blessed the efforts of Dave and a team of faithful pastors in Arvada, Colorado.

> In 2006, I was serving as a pastor at Foothills Community Church in Arvada, Colorado. It is a great church, and we were in a season of significant numerical and spiritual growth. However, I wasn't doing well personally. I was struggling to reconcile what I was doing day to day with a passage of scripture that I just couldn't get out of my mind. Right before He is arrested, Jesus prays a prayer that is found in John, chapter 17. After praying for Himself and for His disciples, Jesus prays for us. His prayer at that crucial moment was that there would be unity between those that call themselves followers of Him. And He doesn't just pray for unity for the sake of unity. He states that when there is unity among His followers,

people that don't know God will be drawn toward Him! I kept thinking to myself, "What if that is true?"

I quickly learned that there were other pastors in my community who also had a passion for unity among the body of Christ. We began to gather to pray, dream, and discern how we might work together to do something together that we could never do alone. A big part of this discerning process involved listening to our city leaders. Fast forward three years to 2009. I was sitting in a room with twenty plus other pastors and our mayor. We asked him if he had any ideas about what we could do together to make an impact in our city. His answer was stunning. Without knowing it, he told us that if we wanted to really serve our city then we should get the people in our churches to actually do what Jesus said to do . . . to know and care about their literal neighbors.

I have since learned that most civic leaders are firm believers in neighboring. They know that it is the key to solving a number of the systemic issues that they are dealing with on a regular basis. As our mayor and assistant city manager say, "Relationships always trump programs."

That conversation with our mayor sent my fellow pastors and myself on an incredible journey. We started by making a commitment to slow down a bit and become better neighbors ourselves. This was huge for me personally. As a pastor I had drifted into a place where most of the people that I spent time with were fairly homogeneous. They thought about the world and about God the way I did. I quickly realized that neighboring is the antidote to the "Christian bubble." As I leaned into relationships with my neighbors I found that my new friends didn't think like me at all. I loved it.

Our pastors' group also began to encourage and challenge the people in our churches to take small steps with the people that God has placed around them. Our rallying cry became, "What you do in your front yard counts . . . it's real ministry."

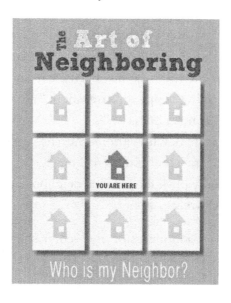

The tool that we used to do this is a very simple block map. It looks like a tic-tac-toe board and has space to write in the names of your eight (8) closest neighbors. When we started using it, we had no idea how powerful it would be for those that decided to use it. So much of the momentum is just getting started. And the block map helped people take a first step. Simply learning, retaining, and using the names of our neighbors can make a huge difference. If you are willing to do that, you will be on your way to taking the second half of the Great

Commandment literally and seriously. If you would like to download a block map for free, please visit the Art of Neighboring website (www.artofneighboring.com).

What has happened over the last six (6) years has surpassed anything that I could have ever imagined. What started with a group of twenty-two churches in a suburb outside of Denver has now spread to over 2,000 churches in twenty-plus countries. Over 250,000 people have made a commitment to literal neighboring and have a block map on their fridge. I believe that one of the reasons for this is because the message has been clear and simple. We just keep asking people this question: "What if Jesus meant our actual neighbors too?"

Through our work with various churches we have noticed that there are a few common characteristics among those that actually push the value of neighboring into the DNA of their church:

1. The primary communicator and senior staff actually do it in their own neighborhoods. This is crucial and if it doesn't happen, then a sustainable movement in the church is very unlikely.

2. Churches that do this well tell stories about neighboring from the front on a regular basis. If you want to cast vision then celebrate what is already happening.

3. When you feel like you are being too repetitive, keep talking about it! This is a very simple concept, and it's tempting to feel like you need to move on and say something new and fresh. You don't.

I've come to believe that Jesus is very smart, that when He was asked to summarize the entire Bible, He gave us all a simple strategic plan that has the potential to change the world overnight. The question is this: Are the people that call themselves Christians willing to actually do it?

Finally, we are by no means the first Christian leaders to talk about the value of neighboring. I consider Lynn Cory (the author of this book) to be one of the founders of this movement. I'm grateful for him and for all of the work that he has done in this arena over the years!

THE INCARNATIONAL CHURCH

CHAPTER 20

STARTING A NEIGHBORING MOVEMENT IN A NEIGHBORHOOD
"Can You Imagine the Whole Church Doing This Today?"

Shawn and Carla Caldwell, Acton, California

Our next story is reminiscent of the first-century Church—brothers and sisters of different backgrounds, gathering together in love in order that they might pray for neighbors who have yet to start their journey with Jesus.

> We began our neighborhood ministry by praying for all the neighbors we knew by name. My son Kyle and I (and sometimes Carla, my wife) would walk our street, praying as we went along. We would pray down one side of the street, turn around, and then pray the other side. After a month or two, we reached out to a few of our neighbors who we knew to be Christians and asked if they would be interested in meeting at our house to pray for the neighborhood. The response was very enthusiastic.
>
> At our first gathering, we enjoyed a very simple meal (hamburgers and hot dogs), followed by a discussion that covered a wide gamut of prayer needs for our neighborhood. Everyone prayed after the meal, and

it was then decided that we should try to do this on a monthly basis.

Over the course of the first year, we ran into some difficulty finding a mutually agreed upon time when all felt it convenient to meet, and at times the monthly meeting stretched out to five or six weeks. That became too irregular, so now we gather every third Sunday. Of those who attend regularly, many are of different backgrounds, with only two couples attending the same church.

I can say without hesitation that it has been both a blessing and a blast getting to know our neighbors. We all really look forward to getting together and praying for each other, and for the neighborhood. I do think the meal and fellowship has greatly contributed to the appeal and consistency of our gatherings.

Because we are all of different backgrounds and churches, we don't all agree on everything, but we are definitely united in our belief that praying for our neighborhood is a good thing, and getting to know our neighbors is just icing on the cake.

After little more than a year of our praying together, we decided to invite our un-churched neighbors to one of our monthly meetings. As one would imagine we didn't observe our regular time of prayer together. Even giving thanks for the meal was a bit out of the ordinary for some. Yet God is growing us together into a very close group.

The fact is, I didn't even know most of these people before I started down this path, but now I look forward to seeing them each month. We all enjoy a true sense of neighborhood and community . . . people whose paths might never have crossed.

We continue to pray, waiting expectantly for the Lord to move. After all, this isn't just about making friends . . . it's about leading people toward the Kingdom of God.

CHAPTER 21

TURNING A CHURCH SMALL GROUP LOOSE IN THEIR OWN NEIGHBORHOODS

Jim Lloyd—The Bridge Church, Fresno, California

This next story addresses the transition of a small, inwardly focused group attached to a local congregation into a gathering of missionally minded individuals who had learned to focus on their own individual neighborhoods.

> As a professional educator with almost forty years of experience, the phrase "there is no one way to do this" resonates when thinking about Jesus' statement in Luke 10:27 (paraphrased) "Love God and Love Your Neighbor." I've been conscientious about loving God over the course of my walk with the Savior, but that part about loving your neighbor—not so much.
>
> About three years ago, for a variety of reasons, God got ahold of my heart, and this "love your neighbor" command came alive for my wife and me. It didn't happen overnight, and it wasn't instantaneous; it was a process. As I reflect, God was building a relationship with me and relationships are time-consuming messy, but ultimately rewarding. He was demonstrating in a very tangible way

what I needed to do in my neighborhood. He was calling me to build relationships with my neighbors.

During that process I began to think about how the life group I was leading could be an avenue to reach not only my neighborhood, but also the other eight neighborhoods represented by those attending. After much prayer and discussion with my wife, I took our vision of turning our sermon-based life group into a neighborhood-initiative life group to our pastor.

I shared what God was doing, the new-found passion for our neighbors, and our vision for our life group. Our pastor was enthusiastic, was supportive, and blessed our decision. He also noted others in our church fellowship who shared the same passion, and several life groups began migrating to a "love your neighbor" format.

At this point my wife and I made the unilateral decision to transition our life group to a neighborhood-focused group. Since we take a Christmas break in December then rejoin at the end of January, I used the time to inform each member of the life group about our decision and that beginning in January we would begin focusing on loving those who lived in our own neighborhoods. Each member was given an explanation of our thinking and where God was leading my wife and me. I gave each an opportunity to continue with us or join another life group, whatever direction God was leading them. As it turned out all members of our life group decided to remain together.

Over the next several months we began the journey toward tangibly loving our neighbors. We began reading Lynn Cory's book Neighborhood Initiative. At each gathering we shared stories, experiences, and prayer requests. Life group members were challenged to prayer walk their neighborhoods at least once a week.

In addition, we stressed the importance of mapping our neighborhoods and identifying boundaries within which to operate. We also discussed the definition of a neighbor and decided to focus on where you live, shop, work, recreate, or simply spend time. Future topics will include developing a prayer team of believers from the neighborhood and the power of sharing a meal together.

Remember, there is no one way to do this. I have identified three phases, and I am projecting each phase will last from one to three years. In phase one the focus will be on developing a neighborhood prayer team. The goal will be to identify a committed believer on each block (there are nine blocks in my neighborhood) and encourage them to pray for their immediate neighbors by name, engage in prayer walks, and observe for needs they can meet. Phase two will be to initiate growth groups. A mixture of believers and nonbelievers who show an interest in spiritual things. This is not an attempt to take believers away from their local fellowship or ask them to commit to another night out; rather this phase over three years is intended to introduce neighbors to the kingdom and encourage believers to apply Luke 10:27: Love God and love their neighbors. Phase three is projected from one to three years. During phase three, which I call Life Changers, we will move the group toward focused discipleship and a missional lifestyle.

Remember this is a vision, not my current reality. Will this come to pass? The Lord knows. Will this happen in my projected sequence? I'm laughing now . . . . It will happen as I listen to the Holy Spirit, take advantage of those *kairos* moments, and live in obedience.

CHAPTER 22

STARTING A NEIGHBORING MOVEMENT IN A HOUSE CHURCH NETWORK

Glen Taylor—Vineyard Pasadena Community Church, Pasadena, California

One obvious way to begin neighborhood ministry is to establish a network of house churches. The following comes to us from Glen Taylor, a former missionary to Central Asia for twenty-three years.

Doing neighborhood home church has been one of the most satisfying experiences I have ever had. Our vision is to multiply home churches, neighborhood by neighborhood, in order to participate with God in a grassroots transformation of Pasadena, the urban parts of East Los Angeles, and the world. There are a number of reasons for home church, including the values and priorities of relationship, transformation, neighborhood mission, and leadership development.

For many years I've started home churches in Muslim countries because it was not possible to establish a conventional church. I was well aware that the early church met in homes and grew exponentially. As a naturally task-oriented person, I went through a long process of coming to understand that relationship takes priority over everything else I do. This process of valuing relationships came as I began to understand the implications of what it meant that all people are inherently valuable because of being made in God's image. I also realized that when we leave this world we take only two things: our relationship with God and with people. This was coupled with living for years among and learning from cultures that place relationship above task. The cultures that most deeply impacted me were the Mexican, Turkish, Iranian, and Tajik cultures. This hasn't meant that I don't value organization or action steps. It's simply that relationship is prioritized above all. A smaller home church model makes it easier to live out the value of relationship. Rather than a lot of time and energy focused on sustaining large buildings and complex programs, there is greater focus on developing grassroots relationships.

The priority of relationship has implications for other critical areas such as transformation and mission. I have always been deeply impacted by the Bible's emphasis on a lifestyle of personal transformation and mission. These twin life-rhythms create the adventure and excitement of living in God's Kingdom. I have been frustrated with the inefficiency of conventional church models for producing a high percentage of disciples genuinely living a life of transformation and mission. Learning to live such a life normally requires ongoing face-to-face accountability and encouragement with people who know you well and help you to flourish, grow, and change. I experienced this in home churches overseas. So it was a comfortable model to use in Pasadena and Los Angeles. The small, more intimate, home church setting also facilitates leadership development because at the core of leadership and character development is close, accountable relationship.

The focus of our home churches on neighborhoods came as a result of a combination of valuing relationship with unchurched people and the missional understanding that the second part of the greatest commandment to love our neighbor literally means to love our neighbor! This has a broader metaphorical meaning as well, but in its essence it means literally what it says. Dallas Willard's introduction to the *Neighborhood Initiative and the Love of God*, as well as the short, practical stories about neighboring, have been deeply helpful and encouraging. Other books like the Art of Neighboring have also helped. We nurture the understanding in each home church member that their neighborhood is their parish. We seek to develop and sustain this in a variety of ways: I send out a weekly pastoral newsletter through social media and e-mail in which I share my own missional neighboring experiences for that week. We give a copy of Neighborhood Initiative to each visitor and require that all leaders read it. At our weekly home church gatherings, and our once a month corporate worship gathering, we ask a member to share a neighboring story from that week. Each week in home churches and in my pastoral letters I encourage our community to take a ten-minute prayer walk once a week through the neighborhood and pray for all the neighbors in all the homes they pass and greet anyone they pass on the walk. At our weekly intercession gathering we pray over our neighborhoods. We are involved in other missional ways in our community, but neighboring is the bread and butter. Typically we do not schedule more than two gatherings each week so that time is free to spend with neighbors and unchurched people. We are always learning and growing, but we find that through the smaller home church model we have a much greater participation of our members in missional neighboring than what would happen in a more conventional church model.

CHAPTER 23

PLANTING A CHURCH WITH A NEIGHBORING APPROACH

Joe White—Neighborhood Church, Fresno, California

Here's the story of one young pastor and his family who have taken a most unique approach in defining the neighborhood boundaries of ministry, and in so doing, challenges us to ponder not only our definition of church, but to reconsider the parish model of old.

> Neighborhood Church is not your typical church. We don't occupy a traditional church building. We don't function as one would expect a conventional church to function. Instead, we have "staked out" a specific neighborhood in the city of Fresno where we hope to reflect and manifest the Kingdom of God to those who call this neighborhood "home."
>
> There are 923 homes in our neighborhood, some of which have been taken back by financial institutions. There they sit, empty and boarded up. As for the remainder of the neighborhood, many of the families have been hit hard by the current economy. Of the 3,500 residents, a significant percentage are migrant farm workers, with 71 percent not even having a high school diploma. We experience 18 percent unemployment within our neighborhood, with many more under-employed, and I regret

to report that there are some who have resorted to illegal activities as a result of their hardship. This is our "home": high unemployment, a high crime rate, but fertile ground for the Holy Spirit.

Before I go any further, I need to point out that my wife and I made the conscious decision to not separate ourselves from those to whom we felt called. We believe that ministry should be incarnational. Thus we moved into the neighborhood with the attitude that this was our "flock"—lost sheep in need of the Shepherd. We didn't come to preach or teach. We came to reflect the life of Jesus in such a way that the entire neighborhood would be impacted for the better. And since making that commitment to live in the midst of the "sheep," we, and our neighbors, have experienced God in some powerful ways.

With such a high unemployment rate, the children of our neighbors often experience barriers to employment. One of our dreams has been to repurpose a dilapidated workshop in our neighborhood and turn it into a place where neighborhood teenagers could be paired with Christian mentors who are skilled woodworkers, welders, and artisans. Not only would they learn a trade, but they would learn about Jesus at the same time.

Of course, the reality of coming up with the funds to purchase the necessary equipment seemed to put this dream out of reach . . . that is, until God introduced us to John.

John contacted us because he had heard about our vision for a neighborhood-focused church. We met the next day, and here's the story he shared: "Ten years ago, my passion was motorcycling. I had a beautiful Harley that I loved to ride. One night while sleeping I had a dream. In my dream Jesus came to me and said, 'You need to give away your motorcycle.' I woke up feeling convicted, but I just couldn't give it up. For three months I resisted God. I loved my motorcycle! But I finally relented and gave it away. Since then my passion has been woodworking. I amassed for myself a garage full of high-end cabinetry-making equipment. Three months ago I was sleeping and I had another dream. In my dream, Jesus came to me just as he had before, but this time He said, 'You need to give away your woodworking equipment.' I woke up feeling convicted. Ten years ago I resisted God, but this time I knew what I had to do. Joe, would you like my woodworking equipment?"

I didn't have to answer . . . God was already saying "yes." A man I had never met was going to give Neighborhood Church nearly $10,000 worth of woodworking equipment to further God's Kingdom in our neighborhood. Today there is a repurposed 100-year-old workshop in our neighborhood being used to teach neighborhood kids about Jesus while they learn a trade.

A Vision of Caring for the Needs of Our Neighbors

Unfortunately, poverty leads to poor eating habits, and many of our neighbors either don't have the money or the education to make healthy dietary choices. As we looked out over our neighborhood, we began to wonder . . . Could we help our neighbors make wiser choices when it came to their food purchases? What if we purchased an abandoned property in our neighborhood and, with the help of our neighbors, created an urban farm that would produce enough fruits and vegetables for all the residents living here?

It seems like fantasy, but we recently shared our vision over dinner with some folks who had moved in across the street only a month prior. They aren't Christians, but they listened attentively as we shared our vision for the neighborhood and for our urban farm. We said, "Jesus loves this neighborhood and everyone in it. He wants our bodies to be nourished by healthy food and our hearts to experience his love for us. Our world says, 'We become what we eat.' But Jesus calls us to become more like Him. When we do that, we'll take better care of our bodies (because he made them with love) and work to ensure everyone has access to healthy food."

We witnessed our new neighbors hanging on our every word. Then they said something that surprised us: "We want you to know that it must be no accident that we've moved right across the street. All the stuff you are talking about is our passion and life's work. We help people set up urban farms all across the world. I currently sit on the board of an organization that does exactly what you are trying to do here in this neighborhood. I know how to set this kind of thing up . . . and I want to tell you . . . we are going to help you with this. We will support you in what you need. I love the idea of this kind of church."

We were floored. God was bringing us into relationship with the very people needed to impact our neighborhood. Right before our eyes, Jesus was building His Church . . . one seed at a time!

A Church Just for You!

The stories of some individuals can speak volumes. One such story is about my neighbor, Manny. Manny works twelve-hour days as a machinist and then drives around the city collecting scrap metal in an effort to make ends meet. His wife drinks too much, but behind the drinking is another story—drug use and violence, some of which we have witnessed first hand. In Manny's mind, any dysfunction within his family can be solved with more money . . . or so he thinks.

The other day, Manny saw me in the front yard playing baseball with my son Josiah. His truck was full of scrap metal. "He must be coming home after a long day of work," I thought. After all, he starts work at 2:30 a.m. and it was now 5 p.m. He stopped his car in front of our house and turned off his ignition. Then he rolled down his driver's side window and yelled, "Hey Joe! Come over here!"

I walked over to the car, now parked in the middle of the street, and before I had the chance to say a word, Manny blurted out in his typical gruff tone, "Joe, you've been here for a couple months now. I have to know . . . what do you do, you know, for work?" I laughed. It's a good question. After all, he does see me around the neighborhood a lot.

"Well, Manny, we are going to start a tutoring club for kids at the elementary school that will emphasize math and reading. We are trying to take an abandoned property in our neighborhood and turn it into an urban farm. And we are starting a church."

His eyes perked up and looked right at me. "Church," he said. "What kind of church?"

"Well," I said, "it's kind of a church for people who don't like church."

I watched as his eyes filled with tears. Turning his eyes up toward me, hands firmly gripped on the steering wheel, he said in a low whisper, "Do you mean a church for people like me?"

"Yes, Manny. It's a neighborhood church, a church of neighbors, just like you."

CHAPTER 24

STARTING A CITYWIDE NEIGHBORHOOD MOVEMENT

Andrew Burchett—Neighborhood Church, Chico, California

All across the country, we are hearing stories of citywide movements that focus on neighborhood ministry. Of course, in pondering such a task, the question will naturally arise, "Where do I even begin?" Here's the story of one such pioneer from the city of Chico, California.

> I grew up on the idyllic street filled with kids laughing and playing, and neighbors sitting on their front porch most every evening. Chico was only a small town back then, and it had a rich sense of community and belonging. It was normal to know your neighbors and borrow that missing cooking ingredient from them, take care of their house when they were on vacation, and connect in relationship. Knowing, loving, and being connected to your neighbors seemed natural. The biggest conflicts we had centered around paying for another baseball that broke a window.
>
> As years passed and I married and moved to Southern California I took the mind-set of loving my neighbor with me. It quickly became clear to us that not all neighbors wanted to have relationship, and others who wanted relationship only invited us over to pitch the latest pyra-

mid scheme. Our open hearts and willingness to connect paid off when our neighbor had a brain aneurism and we were able to share the Gospel with the family as well as our lives. We babysat their kids and learned from this couple that was a bit older than us. There were many seeds sown in their lives in that season.

When I moved back to my hometown with a pregnant wife and a heart to love my neighbors, we purchased our first house. At this point, we took cookies to our new neighbors and learned quickly that when you own your home, you are signing up for a long-term relationship with your neighbors. Over the years we have had the thrill of victory arranging block parties and praying with neighbors. Along with the thrill of victory has come the agony of multiple defeats. Some of our most painful moments have been with our neighbors rejecting us, gossiping about us, and trying to sabotage our efforts to make a difference in our neighborhood.

Several years ago I heard about a movement of the Holy Spirit across our nation—a movement that was all about neighboring and loving your actual neighbors well. As I was trying to see a vision for the future of our church and for how it would connect with the church of Jesus Christ in the city, "neighborhood initiative" jumped out at me. Since becoming the lead pastor of Neighborhood Church in Chico, California, it has been a key expression of the vision God has written on our hearts.

We have enjoyed learning from other regions and cities that have gone before us, and we are fortunate to have a strong network of Christian pastors in our city who pray and work together. With the help of the "father of our city," Gaylord Enns (who served as a pastor here for over thirty years and helps to gather those serving in ministry), we introduced the concept of neighboring as a kingdom-building mind-set to the senior pastors of our city. Some of the men and women were early adopters and began talking about this movement with their congregations. Others decided to start by having their church adopt the block on which it is situated, thereby resulting in multiple churches turning their eyes outward. Pastors have taken small group leadership teams through Lynn Cory's book (*Neighborhood Initiative and the Love of God*), and most of our pastors have gathered to hear Lynn share his thoughts on neighborhood ministry.

While some pastors have quickly adopted this new ministry focus and have shared it with their congregations, others have felt somewhat threatened by the idea that they might have to cut short some of their church programs in order for their members to have sufficient time to spend with their neighbors. But those churches that envision missional communities as a key part of their outreach strategy have readily incorporated Neighborhood Initiative into their day-to-day ministry.

It has been a privilege for me to help lead the fellowship of local pastors in our city and to help keep Neighborhood Initiative in the forefront of everyone's thinking. As we move forward together, we continue to follow the Holy Spirit's lead, dreaming of the day when a Christian in Chico will be easily identified by the love they extend toward their neighbors. Together we have reached out to the Chief of Police and asked for input as to how we might better serve our city. This has resulted in a sense of "partnership" between the church and local government, allowing us to take responsibility in very tangible ways in our city, yet all the while maintaining obedience to Jesus' command to love our neighbors. We have even joined together to pray walk blighted areas of our downtown area, demonstrating the love of Jesus with all those we encountered, meeting both the physical and spiritual needs of the poor, and thereby adopting new neighborhoods as our own.

CHAPTER 25

THE FRESNO STORY . . . "LOVING OUR NEIGHBORS"

Paul Haroutunian and Alan Doswald—Fresno, California

The story of Fresno's move towards neighboring involves a lot of players over many years. It's the story of a city in the process of being transformed. Here are just a few of the highlights from two men who have been at the center of what God is doing in Fresno for much of the time.

> The population of the combined Fresno and Clovis areas is around 600,000 people. That makes it the fifth largest population center in California, and the largest inland city in the state.
>
> We began our move toward transformation over thirty-five years ago when a group of Mennonite men started praying for our city. This was followed by the 1990s, or "The Decade of Prayer" as we call it. Those prayers of our Mennonite brothers gave birth to Pastors' Prayer Summits, weekly pastor prayer gatherings, Lighthouses of Prayer, City Builder's Roundtable (a monthly coalition of ministry leaders), and PRAY Fresno/Clovis (a citywide movement of prayer).
>
> All that prayer led to some pretty dramatic results. Crime dropped 43 percent from 1995 to 2000, with violent crime dropping to its lowest level in 30 years. Care

Fresno was launched, with churches coming together to serve the needy in apartment complexes throughout our city. And by 2001, several of our local officials were Christian, including the mayor, chief of police and deputy chiefs, county sheriff, fire chief, and city and county school superintendent.

I might also add that in 2000, Fresno was named an All-America City for how its people were working together to improve their city. And although this was a great result to all our prayers and hard work, we began to realize that transformation was not a destination, but rather a journey that never ends. Many people had been helped and many had come to Christ, but our community had not yet been transformed.

Over the years we've had several large Christian events in our community including three Billy Graham Crusades, a Luis Palau Crusade, and several Promise Keeper rallies. These events were great and helped many people, but they did not transform our community.

With time, and after a lot of prayer, we concluded that events would not transform our city. The transformation of Fresno must be rooted in our lifestyle, and not a series of events.

The lifestyle we chose was modeled after Mission America's motto of Prayer-Care-Share. This had the greatest appeal as it was grounded in prayer and encompassed Jesus' command to love our neighbors.

We thought that we could learn this lifestyle better together, so we formed the Loving Our Neighbors team, a team of like-hearted pastors who were committed to mobilizing and equipping their people to intentionally love their neighbors. We meet regularly to strategize on how to do this best, and once a quarter we open up our meeting and invite other leaders to join us.

Now we feel as though we are making progress toward transforming our city. Pastors are getting on board with the concept. As one leader put it, "I'm proud to serve in the Loving Our Neighbors movement precisely because it's not another program, but a long-overdue return to the basics."

CHAPTER 26

SEEDING NEIGHBORHOOD MINISTRY INTO THE SAN FERNANDO VALLEY

Jeff Fischer—Hope Chapel, Winnetka, California

The San Fernando Valley is arguably the largest single region of Los Angeles. Once a patchwork of sleepy bedroom communities, the Valley has grown into a vast network of commercial, industrial, and residential districts. While only a few decades ago it served as a highly desirable alternative to some of LA's more urbanized areas, the Valley has evolved into a huge metropolis in its own right, becoming the home to people of countless different cultures. Churches abound in every neighborhood, yet unity is rare. The task of reaching such a large, multi-cultural area with the message of the Kingdom is daunting. Yet there are many who willingly and lovingly step into the breach. Here's a story from one of the pastors on the front lines.

> When I was first exposed to Neighborhood Initiative I wasn't quite sure how to begin. We had done community outreach before: neighborhood clean ups; Laundry Love (putting quarters in washers and dryers for people in laundromats to bless and share the love of Jesus with them); praying for every household and business in our town by name on the phone; distributing the Jesus Video to our town; participating in our community Memorial Day parade; hosting Christmas banquets and toy give-

aways for homeless families identified by a neighboring elementary school and in partnership with city and neighborhood council offices and chamber of commerce, LAPD, LAFD, CHP etc.; producing city-wide music and social justice festivals that drew thousands of young people; and other assorted outreach into the city. These were all good, but they were time consuming, demanding, expensive, and most importantly, left out the majority of the church. In retrospect, most of what we were doing fell into the category of "hit and run" or "drive-by" outreach and/or evangelism. The main problem was there was no real sustainable relationship with our neighbors for long-term kingdom impact and making disciples in our "village."

I was coming to terms with a need for our church to become more incarnational/missional in our ministry focus. At a weekly pastor's prayer gathering that I facilitate, Lynn introduced us to Neighborhood Initiative. At first he challenged us to reach out to and love our actual neighbors as pastors! Yikes! You mean we have to take the Great Commandment seriously too? It helped that Lynn had his friend Dallas Willard come speak to our pastor's fellowship about the importance of us leading the way. One of the pastors in our crew suggested that we share our stories as a part of our prayer meeting to encourage us toward love and good deeds to our neighbors. When Lynn suggested that before we introduced NI to our congregations that we practice loving our own neighbors first, I was reminded of something Bob Logan said about missional-focused ministry needing to start with lead pastors. He asserted that it didn't matter if pastors were good at it or did it well. In fact, he said that we could be really bad at it, but that the key was doing and sharing our stories (good, bad, and ugly as the case may be). It isn't success that necessarily inspires people, but the risk taken and the honesty of those leading and modeling the way.

So we began. Various pastors started reaching out to their neighbors and sharing their stories each week as we gathered for prayer. There were both some very powerful and funny stories being shared as we struck out to love our neighbors. Michael, a Messianic Jewish leader in our fellowship had a skin-head living next door with a Nazi symbol in his window. "You mean I have to love him?" Jesus never said loving our enemies would be easy! It was exciting to hear the many different ways pastors and leaders were implementing the ideas offered by Neighborhood Initiative into their own lives. We all believed that loving our neighbors as ourselves was at the core of our calling, but many of us had become so busy caring for the church's needs that we neglected to care for our own neighbors. So my wife, Lisa, and I began praying for our neighbors by name with our little son Luke. He suggested that we make brownies for our neighbors and introduce ourselves as we dropped them off to each home. So we did and were a little surprised how open and happy people were to meet some of their neighbors. We followed it up with a post trick-or-treat party for the neighborhood. We served refreshments around the fire pit in our backyard for exhausted adults to chill and talk. On Easter we egged our neighbors! We placed plastic Easter eggs on their lawn with surprises and candy inside along with a note that said Jesus is Risen!

In the meantime, Lisa and I were sharing our stories and challenging the church to follow suit by praying for, introducing themselves to, and reaching out to their own neighbors. Some did, but many felt intimidated. In order to dislodge some of their fears we decided that we would focus our outreach efforts at Hope Chapel on one neighborhood just up the street from our church. We would do it together and model what neighbor-love looks like from a corporate point of view. There is a fairly notorious neighborhood where a couple families in our church live. It is an apartment-lined community ravaged by gang violence and addiction called Cohasset Street. In the past we had sent out mailers and canvassed the area with invitations to attend special events at the church. This time we decided we would go into the neighborhood and get to know the people. We began by setting up a free pancake breakfast on Cohasset Street. We found an area where we could set up enough tables, chairs, and pop-up tents to seat a couple hundred people, put together a planning team, saturated our efforts with prayer by walking the neighborhood in preparation, and handing out flyers and personally inviting everyone we could on Cohasset Street to come out for breakfast and meet their neighbors. Our heart was to connect neighbors, including the gang bangers. It worked! Many people came out of their apartments and ate pancakes together. We set up a prayer tent for people who needed prayer, and we had the opportunity to pray with a few folks. We decided to make this a regular outreach, having a breakfast at least once a quarter augmented with other types of ministry in between such as distributing bakery products (especially bread) up and down the street. At each pancake breakfast, we offered different things: a puppet show about God's love, piñatas for the kids, backpacks for them to color that said Jesus loved them, etc. By the fourth breakfast we decided it was time to share the Gospel with them. So we set up a stage next to the pancake tables and brought in Greg Mead, international missionary and "Strong Man" evangelist who holds the world record for brick breaks with his head! He performed feats of strength and then preached the Gospel. Many people accepted the Lord on Cohasset Street that day. Over one hundred people responded to an altar call by Greg. One of our Hope families started a home group (we call them MiniChurches) on Cohasset Street to care for those who came to Christ at the event. Next time, we brought Greg back again for another pancake breakfast. We blanketed the community with flyers, and this time there were many more who came to a decision to follow Jesus. On that occasion one of the drug dealers came out and said to my wife, "You need to stop doing this, you're ruining my business." So that was an indicator that drug sales had gone down on the street as a result of hearts changed. We also pulled a before and after crime report on the neighborhood, and crime also had gone down over that same period of our outreach. By the time our season of outreach ended on Cohasset Street we had five families coming to our church from that area, which didn't seem like much fruit to us at the time. It was about two years later that some interesting things started to happen. A woman from Cohasset Street who had the gift of evangelism started coming to our church, and she started inviting all of these young people in the neighborhood over to her house for Bible study. She brought them to church, and there were four teenage boys who told us they had come to the pancake breakfasts years before and had given their hearts to Christ at the Greg Mead event. God had a plan for those boys and used us to connect them to Him. Some of them were baptized at our church. In addition, we started a Spanish-language service that has now become a church and has grown from zero to forty-five people, and many of them have come from Cohasset Street. NI made church exciting again!

We are beginning the process of starting neighborhood focused MiniChurches and challenging all of our members to live the Great Commandment and Great Commission in their own neighborhoods. So for us the story continues. What I love about NI is that it serves as a great framework that empowers God's people to fulfill the irreducible core of authentic Christianity. From here we will work to see Hope Chapel and many other churches in our valley work together to reach this great city with God's transforming love: the Whole Church taking the whole Gospel to the whole city one neighborhood at a time.

CHAPTER 27

ONE PASTOR'S JOURNEY INTO NEIGHBORHOOD MINISTRY

Tom Anthony—Oak Hills Church and Neighborhood Collective, San Antonio, Texas

Along with Dave Runyon, Tom Anthony is another pioneer of the neighborhood ministry movement. But, as is sometimes the case, the journey from pastoring an attractional-based church to one focused outwardly on neighborhood ministry can take longer than expected. In Tom's case, his journey spanned four different pastoral assignments.

> I planted a church in 1994 in Indianapolis with limited resources and a very small group of people. In the early years, we dreamed about living in biblical community and reaching neighbors far from God. We were a slowly growing church with a low percentage of transfer growth and a high percentage of conversions.
>
> As the church grew over the next six years, we continued to add more and more people and programs. We went from a church with only a Sunday service and a lot of passion for reaching people far from God to a church with a lot of programs. We became a fast-growing church with a high percentage of transfer growth and a low percentage of conversions.

About that time, our elders spent a year studying (and re-studying) Acts 2:42–47. Our decision was to get back to our roots of living in the neighborhoods and reaching people far from God. Initially, many in the church resisted with some leaving to go to other churches. By the end of my time there, though, we were a church with almost twice as many people in neighborhood groups than we had attending on a Sunday morning. The church was growing and flourishing. My time as a senior minister was over, but my passion for neighborhood ministry was growing.

In 2007, we moved our family of ten to Fort Worth, Texas, to join the staff of Pantego Bible Church. Randy Frazee, author of The Connecting Church, had recently left, but the church was still committed to a ministry built around neighborhoods. I had the opportunity to build and shepherd leaders of neighborhood groups all over the city of Fort Worth. I was surprised one day when one of my neighborhood leaders said, "I know I'm not doing it right. None of my people will probably ever come to Pantego Bible Church."

I asked him to describe what was happening. He said his neighborhood group had grown to over fifty people each Tuesday night, but most of them were far from God and would never drive across town to Pantego Bible Church. People were growing, and others were coming to Christ. For some reason, he had embraced the idea that all of his neighboring efforts were really a way to get people to attend on Sunday morning. I quickly told him to keep doing exactly what he was doing.

For two years, I had the opportunity to work with a

team of people who were committed to building a model of neighborhood ministry in a church of 2,000 people. We had about 100 healthy home groups spread all over the city. What I realized later was this was preparing me for what God had ahead in neighboring.

Two years into my time in Fort Worth, a church in Monument, Colorado, asked me to come on staff to help them transition to a neighborhood model. This was an incredible opportunity to partner with a senior minister committed to decentralizing ministry efforts into neighborhoods. Early on in the transition, we landed on an amazing vision statement. Our vision was "to develop genuine biblical community on every street in the Tri-Lakes region." This was a bigger vision than simply developing geographically based small groups. This was a vision to see neighborhood groups built on every street in the area.

Over the next five years, we made some incredible strides in developing leaders, groups, and vision for being the church in authentic biblical community outside the building. Some of our people resisted, and some left for other churches to continue the programs they wanted. During the next five years, though, our church continued to grow every month and every year. Over that time period, God doubled the size of the church as more people started to embrace the vision for "genuine biblical community on every street."

Five years into my time at Tri-Lakes Chapel (newly named The Ascent Church), I got a call from Randy Frazee asking me to come to San Antonio to help Oak Hills Church transition to a neighborhood model. When he asked me to consider coming, I quickly told him I had no desire to leave Colorado! God, though, had other plans, and He made it very clear we were to relocate once again.

Oak Hills Church is a church of 10,000 on a weekend with three times that many who call Oak Hills Church home. There are thousands of online viewers, and an international presence with the influence of Max Lucado and Randy Frazee. In the midst of this type of size and growth, there is an incredibly high commitment to the neighborhood movement. Our mission and vision is "We are the body of Christ called to be Jesus in every neighborhood in our city and beyond." This is more than just a slogan. The entire church is being built around how to accomplish this God-sized vision.

My team spends every day working on how to help a "gigachurch" move in the direction of being the Church to our neighborhoods and to our neighbors. We have developed a tremendous amount of clarity and resources to help people move in this direction. With hundreds of groups all over the city impacting thousands of people every day, most of us still feel like God is just getting started!

In 2015, two leaders from LifeBridge Church in Longmont, Colorado, partnered with me to begin The Neighborhood Collective (www.neighborhoodcollective.org). An initial group gathered in San Antonio in 2015 to share best practices and learn from each other. This group does not give a one-size-fits-all approach to neighboring. Instead, we bring together like-minded leaders who want to learn from each other and share their best ideas. Leaders all over the country are popping up with a similar heart to be Jesus in our neighborhoods. Getting all of us together in one place is a powerful experience for those who have started the journey with us.

Most church leaders realize the attractional model of church is bringing about limited amounts of true conversion growth. Most pastors . . . in moments of honesty . . . admit their growing church is growing almost exclusively through transfer of Christian adults and child baptisms. Many are beginning to investigate a new way of decentralizing efforts into neighborhoods. Few, though, have the courage to go through with the transition due to the challenges involved. People fear the unknown. They fear change. They fear the loss of long-running programs. The fruit, though, of being involved in the lives of those far from God out in the neighborhoods is undeniable. Most of those who start to experience the joy involved in this type of ministry can never go back to business as usual.

Section 4

Join the Journey

THE INCARNATIONAL CHURCH

CHAPTER 28

ON THE JOURNEY

"One Pastor's Experience on the Neighboring Journey."

John Tolle has been a pastor and church planter for over forty years. He has served both small and large congregations as a senior pastor in addition to functioning in the role of bishop to nearly two hundred churches in the Southern California area. He and his wife currently reside in Thousand Oaks, California, where he pastors a relatively young church plant known as Crosstown Church. From early on, John has made every effort to embed the concept of loving your neighbor into Crosstown's DNA. Because of his vast experience as a church leader, and because he has so ably addressed the challenges we must all face in re-orienting the culture of a congregation toward neighborhood ministry.

> If the truth were known, for much of my pastoral ministry, I had not been a good neighbor. I had given myself a "pass" by rationalizing that my primary ministry was to the local church God had called me to. After all, such responsibility was all consuming.
>
> That all began to change a number of years ago. I had just concluded speaking to seminary students at their chapel service when a professor asked that I stop by his pastoral ministry class to give his students an opportunity to have a question and answer session with a "successful

pastor." Liking the sound of his comment, I obliged.

The Q&A time with the students went well until the third question. The class comedian, who'd already distinguished himself as such, asked the "so, how big is your church" question. A number of his classmates chuckled.

Sensing that this was not his first go 'round asking such a question of a guest, I blurted out, "It's 16,823!"

He was momentarily silenced, but quickly came back with, "Why haven't I ever heard about you and your church?" His blunt comeback left the class in silence and touched a nerve in me.

Why the "16,823" number, you ask?

You see, God had begun dealing with me regarding the many things that I had allowed to creep into my life that defined my ministry. Attendance numbers, programs, properties, money, community events, involvement in missions, evangelistic outreach, celebrity name recognition, speaking at conferences, etc. had all come to identify what a successful church looked like.

Don't get me wrong. Most of what I was doing was good. But the more "successful" I became the further away I drifted from being a good neighbor. Jesus' words of response to those questioning him about the Great Commandment had already begun to challenge my way of thinking:

> *"'You shall love the LORD your God with all your heart, with all your soul, and with all your mind.' This is the first and great commandment. And the second is like it: 'You shall love your neighbor as yourself.'"*
> (Matthew 22:37–39 NKJV)

Being a good neighbor ranked high up on Jesus' chart of importance.

A Shift in My Thinking

My focus as a pastor had been to "get people in" the doors of the church building, not to "get them out" into the world to do the work of the Kingdom of God. I had unwittingly adopted a "come and see" rather than "go, be, and do" the works of Jesus.

The 16,823 number represented a changed way of thinking. It was roughly 10 percent of the population total of our immediate geographical area—a tithe of the valley as we began to term it.

Rather than defining success by the number of people within the four walls of the building, we were to begin caring for people out in the neighborhood. The number was big enough that we couldn't make it a church growth program. Being a good neighbor had to become our lifestyle. We would need to be transformed!

Encouraging People To Be Good Neighbors

Turning an aircraft carrier around quickly is impossible. It takes time. And transitioning people to Jesus' model of being good neighbors will take a lot of it as well.

For me, the following seven items have been God's agenda for our three-year-old church plant. May they be helpful to you.

First, pray for insight! Ask God to help you see clearly where your people are at and how you might teach them to do the ministry of neighboring. Bathe everything in prayer and keep praying.

Second, be decisive! It is important to decide that Jesus Christ called His followers to be good neighbors. One cannot simply add neighboring to the church program and expect people to "get it." A lifestyle change comes from an intentional commitment to Jesus' command.

Third, model being a good neighbor to your people. I had to start being a neighbor in my area so that the people of the church saw it being lived out. I couldn't simply be a talking head. I had to practice what I preached.

Fourth, make room for neighboring. Because most of our people's lives as well as our own are jam-packed with busyness it is important to teach people how to make margin in their lives. Being a good neighbor doesn't happen according to schedule. It happens serendipitously, so it is important to have room in life for the unexpected.

Fifth, be courageous and fearless. Moving out in faith requires big doses of courage. Read all about the ordinary men and women of the Bible who became great for fearlessly stepping out. Fill yourself with the testimonies of others who have challenged their status-quo lives and emerged victorious.

Next, have fun at this new paradigm! There's no need to make being a good neighbor a boring or toilsome ordeal. Find ways to enjoy the journey. Too many Christians seem to have been baptized in lemon juice rather than the joy of the Lord.

And finally, stay at it! The people and the process take time. The title of Eugene Peterson's classic book comes to mind: A Long Obedience in the Same Direction. Real incarnation takes time, and the results will be phenomenal!

Congregational Response

Well over sixty percent of the church's present constituency are long-term followers of Jesus Christ—more than ten years as a Christian. Their loving commitment to Jesus is profound! Their willingness to serve is unmatched; their participation in our worship services is superb. I could go on and on about their great qualities. But I must say, and most of the people would agree with me, that we aren't very good at impacting our hurting, hopeless, and lost world. But that is changing!

Challenges We've Faced

Being the kind of neighbor Jesus calls us to be is not easy. It involves radical obedience—real honest-to-goodness obedience.

It has become apparent to me that we have excluded important matters in our discipleship models. Most of them have focused on knowledge of the Word of God, participation in the local church, and learning the great disciplines of our Christian faith. These are all fabulous and important! However, many of us have failed to mobilize our people to "go and do what Jesus did."

Here are some of the "bumps" in the road we've encountered.

Some people are slow in adopting Jesus' model of going into the world to be good neighbors, but in time they have come around. Others simply have refused to accept their role as a ministering believer. Their argument is the oft heard, "Ministry is your job, Pastor." They have tended to stay at arm's length. And a good number of people are terrified to move beyond their comfort zones. Dealing with their many dimensions of fear in the power of the Holy Spirit has been an ongoing challenge.

Also, helping our people deal with the unexpected realities that come up in neighboring has prompted a doubling down on teaching the principles of walking in the Spirit. Because we are people of habits and formulas, we don't like how people don't fit into our nice Gospel box. Yet it is into such a world that God sent His Son.

Learning and Learning

- I continue to learn and relearn God's ways of pastoral leadership. Among them are the following three insights:

- Being a good neighbor is a priority with God! After all, He sent His son, Jesus, into our world's neighborhood.

- People take time. They always take time. There are no shortcuts. Pastoral leadership requires patience, and guts to lead people where they've never been before.

- God rewards and honors those who persevere. There is a "harvest of blessing" for those who stay with it! No farmer gives up on his planted seed. Neither should we. We'll reap if we faint not.

ON THE JOURNEY

My Own Neighborhood

When my wife and I moved to our present home over ten years ago we didn't expect to encounter what we did. The few people we knew in the neighborhood soon moved out of state. We were left to make friends with the neighbors we didn't know.

Immediately we found out that drug dealing was present in the neighborhood. In fact, someone had been recently shot. Bad blood existed among some neighbors, and the residence on one side of ours was a flop house for a local Southern California rock band that enjoyed partying until the sun came up. It seemed like the police were around a lot. And because people discovered that I was a pastor, a certain "closedness" was apparent among many.

But God has been faithful to give us wonderful favor and has helped us to be on a first-name basis with most of our neighbors. And we've been able to repeatedly pray with many of them, with three having invited Jesus Christ into their lives. People take time and God will open doors.

> *"[God] who calls you is faithful and he will do it."*
> 1 Thessalonians 5:24 (NIV)

The Incarnational Church

CHAPTER 29

STARTING THE JOURNEY
"Moving toward Becoming the Incarnational Church; Leaving the Attractional Model Behind."

The following is my interview of a pastor who asked not to be identified, but is simply referred to as "Pastor Jim." His reasons for doing so should become obvious as you read on.

Though outwardly successful from the perspective of many, Pastor Jim openly shares his struggle with ego, and how his desire to build a church with greater impact in his community began to come into conflict with his understanding of Jesus' command to "love your neighbor as yourself."

We begin with my question concerning the decision to open a second church campus rather than build a larger facility that could easily house the entire ministry.

Q: How did you arrive at the decision to not build a larger facility, deciding instead to have two campuses rather than one?

A: In 2009, we were just filling up our campus and were reaching the functional capacity of our facility. Wanting to stay ahead of the curve, we began having some serious discussions with the elders of our church. There was a certain group that wanted us to build a bigger campus . . . build a bigger sanctuary. But my concern was avoiding what I affectionately refer to as the "Pastor Jim Show." I didn't want it to be about me. I saw that as dangerous for me and considered it to be unhealthy for our congregation. Moreover, I considered it to be unhealthy from a kingdom perspective. Therefore, I proposed that instead of building a bigger campus, that we open a second campus in town, thereby allowing us to train men . . . ideally, younger men than myself.

Q: How did you work out your plan?

A: After identifying some young men, I spent a couple of years training them so that they would be able to teach. During those two years I would go from one campus to the other, leading all four services. Beginning with the third year, I would teach at one campus and one of them would teach at the other. On the following week, we would alternate. In so doing, we began introducing the next generation of leaders to both congregations while reducing my presence. As we have sent men out to plant churches, we have just added another person to that rotation. It has proven to be a very good method for developing leaders generally and developing teachers specifically.

Q: Why did you prefer the two campus approach vs. a bigger building and a bigger congregation?

A: I think it is better for the Kingdom not to leverage my gift or to amplify the gift of any particular leader, because that tends to diminish the development of more leaders. That's just my preference. Smarter men, more dynamic men, more effective men have been very successful at building a bigger barn and seeing it filled. And God, to His glory, has blessed that approach. For me, I think it is healthier for my ego if the growth and development doesn't revolve around me. From my perspective, it shouldn't be about me. It should be all about Jesus.

Q: How do you think one's ego could be fed by having a bigger building and a larger congregation?

A: Look at Jesus' temptations in the wilderness. There are three forms of temptation. The first is pleasure or comfort: "Turn these rocks into bread." The second is prominence or significance: "Hey, jump off the pinnacle and you will not dash your foot . . . Let them know the Messiah is here." And the third temptation is power or control: "All the kingdoms are mine . . . bow down to me and I will give you all of them."

For leaders that seek pleasure, they will give in to the idol of personal comfort. This is, in my opinion, laziness. Others succumb to the idols of prominence and power, wanting to be significant, wanting control. None of us are above those temptations. If we do not consciously bridle our flesh, temptation will win out. And in the circle in which we operate (the church), there can be a tendency to elevate people, especially people on the platform. It can be intoxicating. Intoxicating like the song of the sirens.

Unless we are bound to the mast and bridle the flesh it can lead to our destruction and the destruction of those we are influencing.

Q: How do you know when you are feeding your ego?

A: Well, sometimes I don't. It may start innocently with a question to my wife: "How do you think church went today?" In reality, I'm asking her, "How did I do?" But it just sounds more spiritual to say, "How did church go today?" Or to tee it up with, "Hey, how did you think the worship set went?" And then I can ease into "How was the message?" And I don't even call it "my" message. I call it "the" message. But really what I am looking for is affirmation. And that's just flowing from my own insecurity or my desire to have significance. And so, it can be real subtle in that way. Most of us who have been doing ministry for any period of time have received many accolades for our effort. Our reflex response is, "Glory to God." But inside, we may be thinking, "Yah, I was really good." And I think it takes some time for us to sanctify our lives in the Christian experience where we become more aware of our ego and that desire to have significance and to be influential over others. Having some gray hairs helps in that regard.

Q: What do you think brought you to this place with your ego? Has it always been there?

A: I think growing in Christ has a lot to do with it. I work with a team of pastors in helping to lead this church.

Sometimes I think I am the smartest guy in the room, and it's more than sometimes. That's a very proud thought, and I have to confess it, not only confessing it in the context of your question, but confess it to my friends, to our church. It's an ugly thought. God's given me certain gifts, and I appreciate that. But to not respect the gifts of others, or to think more highly of myself, is sin. This is ugly, and unless I deal with it as I would an idol, it is going to dominate me. Sin is knocking at the door. It wants to dominate me. And unless I address it, it will.

Q: As a successful pastor, why do you feel it is so important to bridle your ego?

A: Presumably, some time within the next forty years, I am going to be in the presence of my Lord, and I am no longer going to be Pastor Jim. I am not going to be someone who had a large sphere of earthly influence. I am just going to be a child of God, and I think it is much healthier for me to realize that now rather than waiting to be on the other side of glory and coming then to this realization.

Q: What do you do to counteract the feeding of your ego?

A: For me, it's been really helpful to create accountability with others. All the things that we're talking about are things I've said publically on the platform at the church where I serve. That establishes accountability with my congregation. I also have a team of pastors that I meet with weekly, and I've had to confess to them as well.

Q: How does your pastoral team respond to your desire for them to hold you accountable?

A: One of the glorious by-products is that they have real respect for my desire to be held accountable. There is a real respect for my desire to decentralize power. There is a real respect for my desire to keep my ego in check, to admit my struggles with these issues and to progress in my personal sanctification. Their involvement in this process is extremely helpful, and they're able to speak into my life at times when my attitude doesn't reflect my values.

Q: Are there others that hold you accountable?

A: I have a few pastors in my life that I meet with on a quarterly basis or every six months, and we have conversations about where I might need to grow in my life. I ask, "Have I made progress? Have I got worse? Has it stayed the same? And what other areas do you see that I need to work on?"

Q: How about your family members? Do they hold you accountable?

A: Yes. I ask my wife, "How can I be a better husband? How can I be a better father to our sons?" And I ask my sons, "How can I be a better father? How can I be a better husband to your mom?" Like any young adult, they see the conversation coming and say, "You're doing great, Dad!" And, Lord willing, that behavior will be modeled for them so that when they are married they will pass it on to their children.

Q: Don't you think that this is one of the most important qualities that we can pass on to our children as well as those in ministry?

A: I think accountability—being vulnerable—is healthy. It is certainly a healthier approach than creating a model where we put our self on a pedestal, where we maintain an appearance of not being mortal, especially with reaching the next generation. From my experience, millennials have a very short tolerance for insincerity, for a lack of vulnerability, a lack of transparency. These are character traits they crave, and I think it is much healthier for the next generation if we model accountability. If we don't, we will see a lack of the intergenerational church. We will see young people separating themselves in order to pursue a more authentic church experience.

Q: What would you recommend for the successful pastor of a large congregation so that ego doesn't get in the way?

A: What I see currently in the church is the phenomenon of "celebrityship," usually associated with the mega-church. We have more mega-church churches of 2,000 or more than we have had at any time in the history of the church. Add to that social media and media in general, and we have all the ingredients to create celebrity-pastor status. We have also seen more celebrity pastors fall, to the amazement of other leaders and to the church in general. So, there is a danger that accompanies this new status. I certainly can't judge anyone, including myself rightly, but I am assuming everyone is trying to bridle their ego. Anyone who doesn't confront their ego and their desire for significance is going to have difficulty navigating the landmines that are inherent with this phenomenon. One can still be very influential in advancing God's Kingdom without seeking personal significance, but that requires having a Kingdom perspective. I've watched men do it and do it remarkably well. But it requires intentionality, accountability, and a lot of work.

Q: Why do you think it is difficult for pastors in a city to come together and operate as one with a common vision?

A: I think there are several things to consider. First, we as pastors are frequently expounding to the church the virtue and value of establishing relationships, when often times we are not healthy at doing it ourselves. Second, there is a lack of respect sometimes for others whom God has called to the same city. Third, there is all too often a level of mistrust among pastors for fear of stealing one another's sheep. And fourth, each local church is unique in its calling, which I believe is correct, but that uniqueness can build walls that keep us apart from one another. I believe that with that uniqueness there comes unique gifting . . . unique passion . . . and a unique sense of responding to community needs. So, in my opinion, each local church should be engaged in both the process of establishing a common vision as well as working out that vision within the community. I believe that to be God's design.

Q: What must pastors do to work together with a common vision?

A: To work in commonality means that we have to let go of some of our own dreams. Our dreams may have to die in order to embrace a common vision that all can embrace. And in order for communities to experience transformation, people need to embrace a common vision.

Q: What has been your experience with working together with a common vision?

A: In my experience, it's challenging. In any partnership, partners are bringing varying gifts to the mix. And sometimes if you feel you are carrying more than your proportional weight, it can breed resentment. So you not only need acceptance of the vision on everyone's behalf, but you need buy-in as well—assurance that everyone will be doing their part. Unfortunately, sometimes getting all of those people working together can be like herding cats.

Q: What is your perspective on large-scale, city-wide initiatives?

A: Some large-scale initiatives by their nature are more time consuming. It takes greater complexity to plan something that is going to take years to implement as opposed to, "Hey let's organize a night of worship at one of our churches or a gathering for prayer for the National Day of Prayer." It becomes much more complex to keep all the pieces working in unity. It takes a very gifted group of leaders to organize and maintain that work by the Spirit of God. The greater the complexity, the more challenging the initiative can become.

Q: Is there any mentoring going on in your city among pastors?

A: We have those who are more mature in experience, and they are encouraged to be proactive in developing relationships with some of our younger leaders. We put the onus on the more mature guys: "Don't wait for a young guy to call you to be a mentor. You have the experience, reach out to them." It's an incredibly healthy thing to do, and I rejoice in it. We have a great sense of unity within our local ministerial association.

Q: What are you envisioning for your congregation as you move forward?

A: I have been blessed to be the founding lead pastor at this congregation for twenty years, and as we celebrated our twentieth anniversary, we began the process of establishing a long-term vision. Because of our stability and size, we're looking forward ten years as opposed to the more typical three or five years. At the end of that period, I will be sixty-seven, and while I would like to think there will still be a lot of tread left on the tire, it would be naive of me if I didn't presume that I will have slowed down somewhat. For the health of the church as we contemplate this vision, we created a team of six core pastors from our congregation that approached the vision with a blank slate. We recognized two things that we have done historically really well that we didn't want to completely jettison, because it is why people are here presently. Those two things are leadership development and spiritual formation.

Q: What insights came from your conversation with your pastoral team?

A: As we contemplated our vision, we realized that our weekend adult attendance is approaching 2 percent of the community at large. Missiologists tell us that two percent is the threshold. If you can reach 2 percent of a population you have, in effect, reached the entire people group. That 2 percent will influence the remaining 98 percent. Applying this to our own situation, our pastoral team recognized that we have the opportunity to reach the entire community. So, as our long-term vision, the pastoral team came up with this idea of saturating our city with small groups.

Q: I understand that you have caught the importance of neighboring. How has it influenced your ten-year

plan, and how does it line up with your value for decentralization?

A: During the conversations with my pastoral team, I have been exposed to different thinkers on the subject of neighboring. Eventually, we got the vision to saturate our city with the Gospel by marrying the neighboring concept with our community group ministry. Being a pastor of what is considered, demographically, a large church, I am always excited about what I describe as a God-size vision. Trying to reach a whole city is something that was attractive to me. It is God-size. The idea of being decentralized—that the plan is not about me—that it is about the person who is leading a neighborhood group as well as the people in that neighborhood group. They're the heroes of this story. They're the ones who are actually loving their neighbors.

Q: How did you personally arrive at the importance of neighboring?

A: I can get so caught up in being about "my Father's business" and actually convincing myself that I am doing my Father's business because of my involvement in administering the programs necessary to support our ministry. But in doing so, I have neglected the clear command of my Lord—to love my neighbor. Jesus said, "This is the key command, love the Lord your God with all your heart, with all your soul, with all your mind and with all your strength, and love your neighbor as you love yourself." And yet somehow I neglected that simple, radical, revolutionary thought by being involved—hyper involved—in doing ministry. I was so oblivious to the obvious that I didn't know I was neglecting the people right around me. I didn't create margin in my life to get to know them, because I was so busy doing "my Father's business." It is no different than the Parable of The Good Samaritan. Yet, I couldn't see it going on in my own life. When that finally sunk in, it was a real "a-ha" moment for me.

Q: As you see it, what are the benefits of a large-scale initiative married to neighboring?

A: One of the things that I think that can be really attractive to a pastor who has been successful in ministry is that he wants to embrace large-scale initiatives. But a large-scale initiative based on neighboring puts a bridle on the ego. For me, as a pastor who has been successful with a large platform, a pastor who wants to contemplate large-scale initiatives for the Kingdom, reaching my community and saturating it with Gospel-centered groups scratches my itch for a large-scale initiative, but because it is decentralized and all about small-group participants, it has by its very nature assured that my influence will be minimized, thereby leveraging the influence of others. Because of this, I can rejoice.

Remember that Jesus told His disciples that they would do greater things than He. And they did! But in so doing, they enhanced their Master's reputation. What Elisha did, enhanced Elijah's reputation. For any large-group, any large-platform pastor who wants their name leveraged, there is something attractive about this. Any of us who want to leverage our name have to come to grips with the fact that He must increase and we must decrease. It wasn't like, "Well, can't Jesus increase, and I can increase too?" No! We must decrease, and I think neighboring allows us to do just that. That's why I am really excited about our congregation's future.

Q: What is your plan moving forward?

A: As I said, ours is a ten-year initiative. We presently have fifty to sixty groups that are primarily based on affinity. What we plan to do moving forward is cast a vision for groups primarily based on geographic proximity. Although, we will not forbid groups to continue that are based on affinity or preclude them from starting, we are going to be constantly talking about the advantages of geographic proximity. In the long run, culture will shift, and I believe that will be healthier for us as a congregation. We like to use the word neighbor as a verb now, and it's going to take time to shift the culture, but all of our core pastors have embraced this vision, and we're looking to simplify programs of ministry in our church. We are committed to this as a vision for ten years. With that much focus and intentionality, we believe it is the leading of the Holy Spirit. We are looking forward to seeing what God will do to make us better followers of Christ.

CHAPTER 30

JOINING THE FATHER IN THE NEIGHBORING MOVEMENT

"A Missionary's Story of Being Invited to Join the Neighboring Movement."

Almost eighteen years ago, I gathered together with more than a million men on the National Mall in Washington D.C., and the Lord spoke to me at the close of the dramatic event with these words from Coach Bill McCartney: "Go back and win your city." Those words, coupled with the Holy Spirit's prompting, impregnated something in me that eventually gave birth to the ministry of Neighborhood Initiative. What God birthed in me through Coach McCartney's words that day has far exceeded anything I could imagine, gathering momentum in one city after another.

As I type this chapter, I am, once again, in Washington D.C., only a few blocks from the National Mall where thousands will gather for Together 2016. As I ponder how God is using so many in the neighboring movement, I look with anticipation to see those He will use next. God loves to use people who are willing to die to themselves and are willing to say, "Speak, Lord, your servant is listening" or, "Here am I Lord, send me." It is so easy to hang on to the familiar, but it is only when we willingly surrender ourselves to Him that the Spirit can bring forth the fullness that He has planted within us.

THE INCARNATIONAL CHURCH

Over a year ago, Lyle told me that he had given one of the Neighborhood Initiative books to a missionary friend of his who had just returned to Los Angeles after serving for nine years in Uganda. In the flesh, I wanted to call and get her response to the book. But the Lord clearly spoke, "Don't call her!" Not long after, I flew to Houston to lead a workshop on neighboring at a Mission America Coalition Leadership Consultation. What transpired reveals just how deeply involved God is in patching together a network of like-minded, fully surrendered individuals who are open and willing to be used by Him as He initiates this neighboring movement among His people.

I arrived in Houston with a couple of my neighboring buddies, Alan Doswald from Fresno, CA, and Fred West from Lake Elsinore, CA. During the months prior, the three of us had planned out our Loving Neighbors Workshop and who would teach what. Each of us approached the opportunity with great anticipation. We all agreed that it was important that we hear first from those who were in our workshop. We let the group know that we wanted each of them to give their name, where they were from, what ministry they were a part of, why they were in the workshop, and what their passion was for neighboring. I turned to a woman on my right, just a short distance from me, and asked if she would go first. With exuberance, she said, "I am Dr. Linda Marcell. I am from Los Angeles, California. I am a part of Faithful Central Bible Church in Inglewood, CA, and I lead an organization called Agape Global Missions. I returned last year from Uganda where I was a missionary for many years. I am in the workshop because I am interested in neighboring. I am presently reading Lynn Cory's book, Neighborhood Initiative, and I have a growing interest in neighboring." I don't believe at this point she realized that I was the same Lynn Cory who wrote the book. I said to her, "I think I know who you are. Do you know Lyle Randles?" She responded, "Yes, I do!" We both laughed. At that point, the light went on . . . we both realized that God had orchestrated this amazing moment far away from home. The whole group was caught up with what God had done, and I sensed His presence in the room. The two of us probably live an hour away from each other, but the Lord had in mind that we would travel over 1,500 miles to meet one another. You can't make these things happen. Someone pointed out to me that if I would have called her before we left for Houston I would have ruined what God put together that day.

After the conference, I traveled back home. However, Linda stayed an extra day in order to catch a flight the next day to Dallas, Texas. A couple of days later, much to my surprise, I received a call from Linda. She was now in Dallas. Filled with joy, she said, "I now know why I came back from Uganda! I spent the whole day in my hotel room praying and reading your Neighborhood Initiative book cover to cover. I now know that the Lord brought me home to be a part of Neighborhood Initiative."

Linda is deeply rooted in the love of God and has a passion for prayer, discipleship, and evangelism. Since the day I talked with her on the phone, she has not stopped teaching others the importance of neighborhood ministry.

I thank God for Linda and all of the others out there like her who have heard God's call and have joined the Father in what He is doing in the neighboring movement. I am constantly hearing of more and more people, pastors and leaders, churches, and citywide movements that are entering this beautiful work that God has initiated.

Is the Lord speaking to you as He did to me on the National Mall, or as He did to Linda in her hotel room in Houston? Is the

Holy Spirit impregnating you with a seed that is growing in your heart for neighboring? Merely say, "I hear You, Lord, send me, show me what You want me to do. Let me join You in what You are doing in my neighborhood and my community."

Notes

1. Lynn Cory, *Neighborhood Initiative and the Love of God* (Colorado Springs, Colorado: NavPress, 2013), 9.
2. Phillip Yancey, *Vanishing Grace* (Grand Rapids, Michigan: Zondervan, 2014), 35.
3. Lynn Cory, *Neighborhood Initiative and the Love of God* (Colorado Springs, Colorado: NavPress, 2013), 10.
4. George Barna, from the Barna Study, www.barna.org
5. George Barna, from the Barna Study, www.barna.org
6. Dallas Willard and John Ortberg, *Living in Christ's Presence* (Downers Grove, Illinois: InterVarsity Press, 2014), 111–112.
7. Robert Jamieson, David Fausset, A. R. Brown, *Jamieson, Fausset, Brown Bible Commentary*, vol. 3 (Grand Rapids, Michigan: William B. Eerdmans Publishing, 1935), 244.
8. Shahkrokh Afshar, Shahzam Factor Blog, *Why So Many Dones and Nones?* May 30, 2016) http://shahzamfactor.com/blog/.
9. Dallas Willard, *Spirit of the Disciplines* (New York City, New York: Harper Collins, 2009), 189.
10. Dallas Willard and Gary Black, Jr, *Divine Conspiracy Continued* (New York City, New York:Harper Collins, 2014), 299.
11. Quoted in Marshall Shelley, *Heart & Soul, Leadership Journal*, September 18, 1996, (accessed July 17, 2015)
12. Jay Pathak and Dave Runyon, *The Art of Neighboring* (Grand Rapids, Michigan: Baker Books, 2012), 23–24.
13. C. S. Lewis, *The Screwtape Letters* (New York City, New York: Macmillan, 1968), 3.
14. Bruce Atkinson, *Land of Hope and Glory* (London England: Dovewell Publication, 2012), 5.

15. Burk Parsons, *"Give Me Scotland, or I Die,"* Ligonier Ministries, http://www.ligonier.org/learn/articles/give-me-scotland-or-i-die.

16. Arthur Wallis, *In the Day of Thy Power* (Fort Washington, Pennsylvania: CLC Publications 2010), 112.

17. Harold Begbie, *The Life of General Booth: The Founder of the Salvation Army*, vol. 1 (New York City, New York: Macmillan, 1920), 84.

18. J. Edwin Orr, *The Light of the Nations* (Eugene, Oregon: Wipf & Stock Publishers, 2006), 103-105.

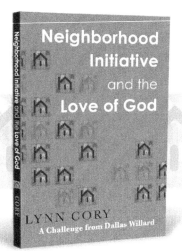

Join a revolution!

What if Jesus' disciples actually demonstrated obedience to His commands that we love our neighbors and one another? Imagine the whole church in every community in our cities working together to bring the love of God to every neighborhood. What if each of our homes became centers for the loving ministry of Jesus? What if every one of our neighbors then began to experience the extravagant love of God? People would say, "I want to have the kind of love they have! And Jesus would be pleased."

Through the love and power of the Holy Spirit, we can and will see this in our day. Neighborhood Initiative is for those who want to join a Jesus revolution of love in our cities, neighborhoods, families, workplaces, and schools.

Order Books:
Neighborhood Initiative and the Love of God and The Incarnational Church at neighborhoodinitiative.com.

If you would like more information about Neighborhood Initiative or access more resources:
visit us at neighborhoodinitiative.com.

Like us on Facebook:
facebook.com/neighborhoodinitiative

Follow Lynn Cory on twitter
@CoryLynncory

Contact Lynn Cory:
lynncory@neighborhoodinitiative.org

Made in the USA
Monee, IL
24 June 2020